S0-FCS-736

Anthropology and the United States Military

Anthropology and the United States Military: Coming of Age in the Twenty-first Century

Edited by

Pamela R. Frese and Margaret C. Harrell

palgrave
macmillan

306.27
A628

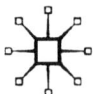

Anthropology and the United States Military
© Pamela R. Frese and Margaret C. Harrell, eds., 2003.

All rights reserved. No part of this book may be used or reproduced in any manner whatsoever without written permission except in the case of brief quotations embodied in critical articles or reviews.

First published 2003 by
PALGRAVE MACMILLAN™
175 Fifth Avenue, New York, N.Y. 10010 and
Houndmills, Basingstoke, Hampshire, England RG21 6XS
Companies and representatives throughout the world

Palgrave Macmillan is the gobal academic imprint of the Palgrave Macmillan Division of St. Martin's Press, LLC and of Palgrave Macmillan Ltd. Macmillan® is a registered trademark in the United States, United Kingdom and other countries. Palgrave is a registered trademark in the European Union and other countries.

ISBN 0–4039–6297–9 hardback
ISBN 1–4039–6300–2 paperback

Library of Congress Cataloging-in-Publication Data
Anthropology of the United States military / edited by Pamela R. Frese and Margaret C. Harrell.
    p. cm.
    Includes bibliographical references and index.
    ISBN 1–4039–6297–9—ISBN 1–4039–6300–2 (pbk.)
    1. Sociology, Military—United States. 2. United States—Armed Forces—History—21st century. I. Frese, Pamela R. II. Harrell, Margaret C.

UA23 .A6827 2003
306.2'7—dc21   2003041437

A catalogue record for this book is available from the British Library.

Design by Ann Weinstock.

First Edition: October, 2003
10 9 8 7 6 5 4 3 2 1

Printed in the United States of America.

This book is dedicated to

All the military wives who helped make this book possible, especially my mother, Edith C. Frese; and Simon, James and Selena, and R.J.

Pamela R. Frese

Mike, Clay, and Tommie, for your love and support; and my favorite Army wife, my Mom.

Margaret C. Harrell

University Libraries
Carnegie Mellon University
Pittsburgh PA 15213-3890

Contents

Preface

John P. Hawkins

W ith this volume we celebrate a kind of coming of age: that of the anthropology of the U.S. military. Anthropology establishes its data by closely observing daily life in societies around the world and by teasing out the meaning of symbols embedded in this flow of behavior and conversation. In this volume, we begin to see the outlines of distinctive military culture and society through the application of anthropological methods. In a word, we begin to see an authentic anthropology of the military.

Every academic discipline or subfield has a history that begins earlier than the first university professional practitioners. For the anthropology of the military, such starting points might include Sun Tzu of China, writing at about 500 B.C. (Phillips 1985), Ardent du Picq of France, writing between 1868 and 1870 (Phillips 1987), or Carl von Clausewitz of Prussia in 1832 (Howard and Paret 1984). These, of course, are theorists of military strategy who came to recognize that success on the battlefield lay not in numbers and weapons, but in organization, orientation, leadership, speed, flexibility, deception, surprise—all matters influenced by culture and cultural difference. Moreover, hundreds of diaries and memoirs record the experiences of soldiers of all ranks, both in war and in peace. From these we can glean hints with which to reconstruct the face of military life in the past. But such works are different from professional, trained, theoretically motivated writings by anthropologist observers.

Ralph Linton (1924), the first anthropologist to my knowledge to study the military professionally, wrote "Totemism and the AEF," an analysis of military insignia and group identity formation during World War I. A group of sociologists and anthropologists surveyed the military during World War II, and, after the war, produced the monumental *American Soldier* studies

(Stouffer 1949a,b). Though survey techniques predominated in this work, they used many quotes from less formal open interviews.

Today we find only a few book-length ethnographies that examine military units or military communities, whether in peacetime or in combat. Roger W. Little spent over four months observing a front-line unit living out of foxholes and trenches on a ridge in Korea during the heat of combat. Described in detail in his thesis, and abridged in an essay, Little (1955, 1964) insightfully documents the formation of social relationships and unit culture and practice that helped create a sense of camaraderie and security within the horror of the war. In rich detail, Charlotte Wolf (1969) described a community of American military advisors in Turkey. Tiring of repeated survey administration, the psychologist Larry Ingraham (1984), a military research officer at Walter Reed Army Institute of Research (WRAIR), employed anthropological participant observation and interviewing to conduct a study of drug use in an American barracks. The methods yielded a rich trove of sociopsychological insight into the processes of alienation among the junior enlisted. Two anthropologists, David H. Marlowe as director and Joel Teitelbaum as participant, collaborated with others to produce the New Manning studies, written up in technical reports distributed by the Walter Reed Army Institute of Research (Marlowe et al. 1985, 1986a,b,c). These reports trace the beneficial impact (and unintended consequences) of COHORT manning, in which soldiers were kept in operational units for as long as possible without rotation, resulting in increased military cohesion and technical proficiency. Pearl Katz, for a brief time also an anthropologist with WRAIR, succeeded in establishing empathy with sergeants and spouses to produce studies of considerable cultural depth (1990). Anna Simons published *The Company They Keep* (1997), a descriptive study of life within Special Forces units. I recently published *Army of Hope, Army of Alienation: Culture and Contradiction in the American Army Communities of Cold War Germany*, a study of family, community, and soldiering in the United States Army enclaves of Germany (Hawkins 2001). In this work I detail the tensions among American culture, institutionalized military culture, and the families must manage their lives in the light of both sets of cultural rules within the enclave military communities.

The scholars in this volume, a new cohort, likely constitute a large percentage of today's anthropologists of the U.S. military. Their work bears on a number of issues that currently stimulate anthropological thought. First, all but one (Guilleman's analysis of anthrax vaccines) explore current postmodern issues: How is anthropology or how are anthropologists accepted, viewed, engaged with, or manipulated by the people studied, and how do we view ourselves in this endeavor?

Chapter 1, by Robert Rubinstein, bears on issues raised in Bourdieu's *The Logic of Practice* (1990). Rubinstein examines how a new cultural logic emerges from the practice of a newly imposed military mission, that of peacekeeper. He also treats practical and ethical field issues: How does anthropology function in military contexts? Why does the social science research community pay so little attention to important and powerful military institutions?

From Marcel Mauss (1936) to Mary Douglas (1978) and Pierre Bourdieu (1990:66–79), to say nothing of the flood of such studies in the last decade, anthropology has long been interested in the symbolism of the human body. In this context, chapter 2, by Jeanne Guillemin, uses historical and documentary sources, in the tradition of the recent anthropology of colonialism, to untangle the web of cultural understandings and misunderstandings regarding iatrogenic disease in the military and the relationship between (colonial) military leaders and (subaltern) enlisted soldiers. Guillemin shows a history in which the military acts in ways that sometimes have harmed rather than conserved the fighting force. Against this background, anthrax vaccination—a bodily injection, bodily invasion, uncertain experiment—brings history, bodily integrity, colonial/subaltern, and officer/enlisted relations into a medical anthropology focus. Joshua Linford-Steinfeld, in chapter 5, provides an observational approach to the politics of the body in which he observes Navy personnel in the context of body image and body practice regarding military weight and fitness standards, food values, freedom of choice, cultural order, and military control of the body. The result is a fascinating insight into the cultural dynamics of Navy life and a possible step in the direction of improved treatment of eating and body image disorders.

Clifford Geertz's thick description and contextual analysis of symbols as a way to tease meaning out of culture has stood as the main mast of interpretive anthropology for some years (1973). Chapter 3, by Pamela R. Frese, provides a sensitive Geertzian cultural analysis of home, family, kin, and community, drawn from the life histories of wives of high-ranking officers residing in a retirement community catering to former military personnel. While their images of culture undoubtedly have been idealized through the process of recovering memories late in life, the chapter places senior ranking elite military community and family culture alongside the many studies of kinship around the world done in the tradition of Geertz and Geertz, in *Kinship in Bali* (1975) or David Schneider, *American Kinship* (1968). Frese shows military kinship and family to be a cultural system of considerable richness.

Culture and symbol are not the only interests of anthropologists. So is the social structure of class. Margaret Harrell, in chapter 4, shows that the officer-enlisted dichotomy parallels the upper-class/working-class division in America as these are played out in gender expectations and marital roles. Thus, Harrell's work reproduces the Army variant of the American role and class systems, as described by David Schneider and Raymond T. Smith in their *Class Differences and Sex Roles in American Kinship and Family Structure* (1973). Harrell places the study of Army family and marital roles and army gender issues squarely in the zone of topics and issues that more recently have concerned many anthropologists exploring feminist issues.

Anthropologists have always prided themselves in being comparativists. Even the most determined postmodernists compare societies or social experiences—their own and those of the people with whom they interact—to show how unique a people's symbols, interactions, or histories are. Anna Simons, in chapter 6, follows the comparativist tradition, but with a twist. She shows how similar to each other are the metatasks of anthropologists and military advisors, while not forgetting key differences. Practitioners of both arts share role ambiguity, risk, exchange, and mutual manipulation with the peoples with whom they interact. Significantly, both advisors and anthropologists find themselves misunderstood and distrusted by leaders in their source culture or institution, the members of which believe, quite irrationally, that advisors (or anthropologists) may be going native and can no longer be relied upon or controlled.

Since Franz Boas, to speak only of the American tradition of anthropology, anthropologists have sought to influence public affairs by teaching anthropology as a form of general education. Through teaching, anthropologists have tried to reduce racism, soften the hard edges of ethnocentrism, and promote intercultural understanding. In this tradition, Clementine Fujimura, in chapter 7, examines the Naval Academy's limited course offerings in anthropology and interpretive social science. She links this absence to the unquestioning command structure of Navy culture and society, and shows that an engineering curriculum is more culturally compatible with Navy culture, for its practitioners do things and ask less troublesome questions as they seek to more efficiently deploy their sailors and weapons platforms.

By interpreting the military from these perspectives—culture as symbols, the social structures of class and gender, the cultural management of body-form as symbol, and in other ways—this volume injects into the mainstream of contemporary anthropology an authentic, rich anthropology of the military. It is, indeed, a coming of age.

References Cited

Bourdieu, Pierre. 1990. *The Logic of Practice*. Stanford, CA: Stanford University Press.

Clausewitz, Carl von. 1984. *On War*, Michael Howard and Peter Paret, eds. and trans. Princeton, NJ: Princeton University Press.

Douglas, Mary. 1978. *Purity and Danger: An Analysis of Concepts of Pollution and Taboo*. London: Routledge and Kegan Paul.

du Picq, Col. Ardant. 1987. *Battle Studies: Ancient and Modern Battle*. John N. Greely and Robert C. Cotton, trans. In Thomas R. Phillips, ed. *Roots of Strategy*, Vol. 2, Pp. 8–299. Harrisburg, PA: Stackpole Books.

Geertz, Clifford. 1973. *The Interpretation of Cultures: Selected Essays*. New York: Basic Books.

Geertz, Hildred and Clifford Geertz. 1975. *Kinship in Bali*. Chicago: University of Chicago Press.

Hawkins, John P. 2001 *Army of Hope, Army of Alienation: Culture and Contradiction in the American Army Communities of Cold War Germany*. Westport, CT: Praeger Publishers.

Ingraham, Larry H. 1984. *The Boys in the Barracks: Observations of American Military Life*. Philadelphia: Institute for the Study of Human Issues.

Katz, Pearl. 1990. "Emotional Metaphors, Socialization, and Roles of Drill Sergeants." *Ethos*, 18:457–80.

Linton, Ralph 1924. "Totemism and the A.E.F.." *American Anthropologist*, 26:296–300.

Little, Roger W. 1955. "A Study of the Relationship Between Collective Solidarity and Combat Role Performance." Ph.D. dissertation, Michigan State University.

—— 1964. "Buddy Relations and Combat Performance," in M. Janowitz (ed.) *The New Military: Changing Patterns of Organization*. Pp. 194–224. New York, NY: Russell Sage Foundation.

Marlowe, David H. et al. 1985. *New Manning System Field Evaluation, Technical Report No. 1*. Washington, DC: Department of Military Psychiatry, Walter Reed Army Institute of Research.

——1986a. *New Manning System Field Evaluation, Technical Report No. 2*. Washington, DC: Department of Military Psychiatry, Walter Reed Army Institute of Research.

—— 1986b. *New Manning System Field Evaluation, Technical Report No. 3*. Washington, DC: Department of Military Psychiatry, Walter Reed Army Institute of Research.

—— 1986c. *New Manning System Field Evaluation, Technical Report No. 4*. Washington, DC: Department of Military Psychiatry, Walter Reed Army Institute of Research.

Mauss, Marcel. 1936. "Les techniques du corps." *Journal de Psychologie*, Vol. 32, no. 3–4. Available at: *www.uqac.uquebec.ca/zone30/Classiques_des_sciences_sociales/livres/mauss_marcel/socio_et_anthropo/6_Techniques_corps/techniques_corps.doc*

Schneider, David M. 1968. *American Kinship: A Cultural Account*. Englewood Cliffs, NJ: Prentice-Hall.

Schneider, David M. and Raymond T. Smith. 1973. *Class Differences and Sex Roles in American Kinship and Family Structure*. Englewood Cliffs, NJ: Prentice-Hall.

Simons, Anne. 1997. *The Company They Keep: Life Inside the U.S. Army Special Forces*. New York: Free Press.

Stouffer, Samuel A. et al. 1949a. *The American Soldier: Adjustment During Army Life*. Princeton, NJ: Princeton University Press.

—— 1949b. *The American Soldier: Combat and Its Aftermath*. Princeton, NJ: Princeton University Press.

Sun Tzu. 1985. *The Art of War*. Lionel Giles trans., In Thomas R. Phillips, ed. *Roots of Strategy*, Vol. 1. Pp. 21–63. Harrisburg, PA: Stackpole Books.

Wolf, Charlotte. 1969. *Garrison Community: A Study of an Overseas American Military Community*. Westport, CT: Greenwood Publishing.

INTRODUCTION

Subject, Audience, and Voice[*]

Margaret C. Harrell

Anthropologists emphasize a holistic approach, which is both the hallmark and most important contribution of anthropology to an understanding of any multicultural society. Contemporary anthropologists who focus on the U.S. incorporate a critical awareness of the modern world system and of our positions as researchers in multiple systems of hegemony, including our own position in terms of race, class, and gender. Our volume contributes to this body of research as well as acknowledges the intertwining of institutions and the accompanying beliefs and practices that include kinship systems and residence patterns, politics, and economics. Contributors to this volume explore the blurring lines between "other" and the researcher and question how far we, as anthropologists, should, and must, directly engage the social forces in which our contributors, and ourselves, are embedded.

The Relationship between Anthropology and the U.S. Military

My personal experience as a cultural anthropologist researching and publishing on military matters in the interest of furthering public policy has led me to consider why the military and anthropology are not more immediate bedfellows.

I was already a military analyst at RAND when I returned to the topic of my undergraduate studies and obtained my PhD in cultural anthropology. After all, I believed that my undergraduate training in anthropology was beneficially tinting my military manpower analysis: I was analyzing gender and racial representation, military families and other social issues in the military. And the military offered incredible cultural richness: history, formality, and tradition but also innovation; hierarchy but also social movement; uniformity but also diversity. Even within the U.S. military, the services perceive themselves as considerably different from one another. While Air Force officers fly off to combat, leaving their enlisted personnel behind in relatively safe and secure support positions, the Army and Marine Corps ground units depend heavily upon their young enlisted personnel to fight the enemy directly. On a daily level, Army officers scorn the separation that the Navy promotes among their officers and enlisted personnel, as Navy officers eat in separate and considerably nicer dining areas (wardrooms) from their enlisted personnel. In contrast, Army officers ensure that the young enlisted personnel are fed before the more senior officers move through the same chow line. While there are numerous examples of such cultural differences between the services, however, in character, their traditions are generally more alike than different. Those who have grown up on Army posts may be surprised that the evening cannon and flag ceremony is scheduled at sunset on Navy bases rather than at 1700, but the bugler's notes are familiar.

The military recognizes several reasons for why they need to understand their own personnel better. First, the military invests tremendous resources to train uniformed personnel and in return, hopes to retain these individuals. Soldiering (as well as the activities in the other services) is inherently more of a young man's game and the young force reflects this: over 50 percent of servicemen are in their first five years of service. Nonetheless, the Services strive to retain the right individuals past that first commitment, and to keep well-trained officers for longer periods of time. The high price of retraining and the need for some senior personnel is compelling. Additionally, the military mission requires that these individuals, most of whom are young, perform as trained and as ordered. Thus, disruptions or distractions from their focus on the military mission can be disastrous.

One such distraction is family life. Oft-repeated lore asserts not only that the soldier who knows his family is taken care of is better able to complete his mission, but also that the individual is recruited, but the family is retained, meaning that unless the family is satisfied with military life, the service member will not stay in the military. In other words, the military must ensure that the entire military community is healthy and happy in order to maintain the best performing fighting machine. Observing, diagnosing and resolving issues of social dissension or quality of life thus become fundamental matters of importance. Military sociologists have recognized this need and some are commonly recognized by most military decision makers. Why are anthropologists not as commonly sought? There are many other issues that are both integral to the military and its mission and potentially of interest to anthropologists. The lives and cultures of militaries and peoples the U.S. military must either work with or fight against; the internal machinations of a fighting force that is grounded in a huge bureaucracy; and, the sociocultural variations of the military population itself.

This chapter explores why anthropologists have not permeated military installations to observe and to help understand this rich social and cultural institution, and why the military has not sought anthropologists more frequently to provide valuable insights. This consideration is loaded with my own personal circumstances, but I believe they provide insights into the larger relationship. Subject, audience, and voice provide the frame for this discussion.

Subject

Both theoretic and pragmatic issues emerge when considering subject. The first hurdle is considerable, in that the typical subject matter of anthropology is frequently misunderstood. The lay public generally either confuses anthropology and archaeology or fails to recognize that anthropologists can, and do, research topics within our own borders. For anthropology abroad, whereas the military sometimes see the value of understanding the cultural niceties of their possible destinations, they often limit the potential value of anthropology to a notional guidebook regarding basic interpersonal and dining etiquette. The bigger issues of international understanding are generally consigned to the political scientists who have consumed the diplomatic and foreign policy career opportunities and sometimes seem not to relish anthropologists in their midst.

The subject of the military can be tremendously diverse. The four military services each have their own complexion, mission, and structure. Within each of these services, the rank and pay grade hierarchy again divide personnel who already differ by race and ethnicity. Their spouses' position in society, while not formally pigeon-holed by rank, do exist in an informal mimic of the larger structure. These spouses may also lack English proficiency. Understanding these multiple differences is important in order to avoid the danger of additive analysis, which tends to consider different forms of oppression as á la carte features. In other words, rather than consider these many differences as "further" differences, it is analytically important to recognize that varying combinations of these factors may produce qualitatively different perspectives.

Another implication also results from the acknowledgment of so many permutations of differences, and in some cases, so many layers of oppression. Patricia Hill Collins articulates the "Two prevailing approaches to studying the consciousness of oppressed groups. One approach claims that subordinated groups identify with the powerful and have no valid interpretation of their own oppression. The second approach assumes that the oppressed are less human than their rulers, and therefore, are less capable of articulating their own standpoint" (Collins 1995:526).

The traditional military approach to its people embodied these approaches. The first of these is closer to solipsism in that it represents less of a consciously racist or otherwise prejudiced view (than in the second approach) and more a lack of understanding or perception. Regardless of their ideological motivation, the military leadership has generally taken care of its people (or not) for purely mission-oriented reasons. The old military adage "If we had wanted you to have a wife, we would have issued you one" expresses that families are not only not beneficial to the organization's mission, but potentially deleterious. That the leadership would "know best" for the soldier and the mission is an assertion that if the soldier did dare recognize and acknowledge his own oppression, his military superiors were still not going to entertain his ideas for change or improvement.

Things have changed more recently, however, with an increasingly caring leadership more concerned about "doing the right thing for the service member." (Because now there is an increasing recognition that doing the right thing also has its payoff for retention and performance.) Now their problem, however, is an uncertainty about what the "right things" are and how best to determine and implement policy. This uncertainty is well-founded, as Collins also stated that "While an oppressed group's experiences may put them in a position to see things differently, their lack of control over the apparatuses of society that sustain ideological hegemony makes the articulation of their self-defined standpoint difficult. Groups unequal in power are correspondingly unequal in their access to the resources necessary to implement their perspectives outside their particular group" (Collins 1995:527). In other words, even though the military now has concrete reasons to want to help their people, they often don't know how to do so, due to a lack of understanding about the daily existences and troubles or pleasures of their own force. What an excellent opportunity for anthropologists! Except for a few hurdles . . .

Hurdle number one relates to the difference between an informant[1] and a respondent. Informants are fundamentally tied to the richness of anthropology. We see the world through informants' eyes and they explain relationships, structure, and reality. Respondents check boxes of questions designed by well-meaning survey designers who rarely write the questions in the semantics of the oppressed. The tradeoff is in quality, richness, and time. Time costs money, and investing in developing informant relationships takes time. Military sociologists and other researchers can get answers much more quickly with their survey methods—and respondents. A second hurdle is the more pragmatic funding issue discussed by Rubinstein in his chapter in this volume.

The third hurdle reflects the closed nature of the military. Researchers cannot just begin a research effort; one must gain access both centrally and locally. Besides the need to obtain access to enter an installation (at the installation commander's discretion), military subjects are loath to interact with a researcher who has not exhibited the appropriate authorizations. In my experience, I've had to keep unit commanders informed because spouses whom I've called for interviews will have their service member check my credentials with the unit command. Once they establish that you are official and approved, the level at which you've been approved can also affect their willingness to speak candidly. This approval process can also stymie efforts at cross-service studies or comparisons, as the approval process has to be replicated in each service. Even a letter of introduction that I once carried from General Shelton (then Commander of the Joint Chiefs of Staff) only facilitated each service's process; it did not negate the need for separate approval processes.

Confidentiality is a messy issue that is more frequently endured by those of us who have chosen to study (and publish about) subjects close to home. Protecting those who participate in these studies seems both an ethical and a practical need. After all, would anyone speak frankly if you didn't promise this? Further, in such a litigious society, the risks involve more than just ethical hurdles. However, once central Department of Defense (DoD) offices have granted access, not all of the military leadership appreciates the need for confidentiality. For example, one senior officer who sponsored a study wanted us to tie individual assessments of work proficiency to specific individuals. It is important to note, however, that such disregard for confidentiality is not just exhibited by the military leadership. After my recent book of Army junior enlisted spouses, *Time* magazine wanted me to identify the spouses so that *Time* could feature their pictures in the magazine's coverage of the book.

Individual subjects can also become a burden for anthropologists when we study our own—or at least when we study people who can order our works from amazon.com. I'm sure that other anthropologists have endured the tension of letting subjects read the draft or final work. Sending the final chapters of my women's stories to them for review was extraordinarily angst-producing for me. What if they felt I had misrepresented their stories? Worse yet, what if they felt I had misrepresented them, their very character, morals, personality, word-usage? What if they resented the fact that I portrayed them as young, living in a trailer park, having children out of wedlock (even though that's who they were)? These were all tensions I had anticipated when I began this research. What I had not anticipated, was the maelstrom that would occur after I published the work. The emails and letters from people who resented my depiction of Army life, who believed either that I had con-jured the negative stereotype myself, or that I was applying it universally. That some people would write letters asserting that they had not read the book, but still disliked both it and me. That the media would cover the book and feature pictures of the people that resented it (usually with their arms crossed indignantly). That one woman would actually found a website for people who did not like the book and name it "Visible Women." Actually, I thought the latter was pretty exciting. None of my colleagues at RAND had warranted organized resistance in the form of a website.

As an individual, I grew weary of the tone of some of the letters and emails. As an anthropologist, I was fascinated by the degree to which my book prompted a grass-roots resistance and furthered discussion on the topic. However, as an anthropologist who continues similar research, I am confronted by the degree to which previous work can affect further research. During my next study of military spouses, the letters of introduction shown to the leadership at eight installations, the commands of seventeen units, and mailed to thousands of Army spouses feature me as "Dr. Meg Harrell" rather than "Margaret C. Harrell." Of course I would have acknowledged my rela-tionship to the previous work if anyone had inquired; the intent was to avoid unintentional bias when entering the field. Had anyone inquired, I would have had the opportunity to address his or her concern about the previous work directly. At times how I envy those anthropologists who select subjects from faraway exotic places!

Audience

Besides being somewhat uncertain about the validity of the military as an subject, anthropologists are also frequently reluctant to work closely with the military leadership, much less enter into the sponsorship relationships necessary to gain the access described earlier. Many anthropologists believe that to do so would equate to pandering to warmongers. After all, many anthropologists are extremely liberal in their politics and world views. In their minds, the defense world is not to be trusted and certainly not to be endorsed. In actuality, if DoD attended AAA meetings and heard the negative attitudes and assertions about the military, many of which were misinformed, DoD would not entertain such a relationship either—not because DoD shirks from criticism, but because they would not respect the lack of information or the irrationalism upon which many such negative opinions appear to be based.[2]

The concept of audience pervades research that's been approved within a DoD context, as the approval process itself and the letter of introduction often specify the reason for the study and thus the eventual audience. For example, Congressionally mandated studies are assumed to be conducted for the highest level of audience. This concept of eventual audience often encourages participation and even candor. For the most junior personnel, the notion that a Congressman will hear their voice is often sufficient for them to participate wholeheartedly. This reaction differs by Service, however, and the Marines stand separate in their reaction to a presumed audience. Almost without exception, every Marine that I have involved in focus groups or interviews has not cared whether Congress, the Secretary of Defense, or the Chairman of the Joint Chiefs of Staff have approved the study. Unlike other service members, they do not ask whether I have published other reports or who has read my previous work. Before they agree to participate, Marines want only to know that Headquarters, U.S. Marine Corps has approved my presence and their participation; their focus is entirely within their own Marine Corps.

The intended audience can also limit the distribution or publication of analysis of the military, which is an unfamiliar constraint for academic anthropologists. If DoD has granted funded and/or access to the subjects, then they often retain the right to review the product and to determine who can read the final work. At its best, this process simply ensures accurate depictions of factual material. At its worst, this process is a political tool to limit the outside knowledge of, or to color the perception of, the military.

Voice

It is sometimes difficult to separate completely the concepts of audience and voice. Voice can reflect the researched subjects, the independent researcher, or others. The style of voice can reflect the prestige, education, gender or ethnicity of an individual, inside knowledge of an organization (such as by using military acronyms) or the authority of a discipline. For many written works, the voice selected reflects the intended audience. But should it always do so? Certainly many audiences have preconceived notions of what valid, credible work should sound like. I assert that DoD uses a unique voice, replete with acronyms and semantics unique to the military and that it also does anticipate and expect a particular voice which must include enough DoD unique terms and quantitative measures to be considered authoritative.

My most recent work highlighted these expectations. *Invisible Women* presented the oral histories of three women. The stories of these women leap from the page with a broad scope of emotions. Additionally, the range (or lack) of maturity, education, socioeconomic backgrounds and other attributes of these young women are readily apparent in their syntax. This work had only limited amounts of numerical facts, few statistics, and no graphs of complicated functions. One very senior policymaker told me that despite the hundreds of interviews with others in the military community, the final book was "only three stories." Thus, he was very unsure about the degree to which one could depend upon the book. He was actually undermining ethnography, although it was not a term or method he recognized.

After initial uncertainty, the senior DoD ranks decided to applaud the book. The richness of the stories, they claim, provide them insights into the lives of junior enlisted personnel that they could not otherwise achieve. The readability of the book supports its broad distribution. I received an email from the same senior policymaker revoking his earlier uncertainty about ethnography and congratulating me on the book's success and usefulness. How interesting that the voice of the book almost guaranteed its failure and yet was also the element of the book that ensured its value to policymakers. In this case, while DoD expected a particular voice they—after considerable hesitation—did embrace a voice novel to them. It's not clear to me, however, how consistently DoD or other new audiences might embrace unexpected voices. To the extent that anthropology is perceived to be a "fun read" but less generalizable, and thus less credible, dependable, and useful than sociology and other disciplines, we are limited in the contributions that anthropology can offer the military. Until DoD and other audiences decide to expand their expectations for voice, this may be a cubbyhole we cannot escape without fundamentally sacrificing the very richness and value of our work. Yet the opportunity is there, to assist the military in improving their mission performance and the way they treat their own. Both this opportunity and the intrigue of the military as a rich and relatively unexplored anthropological subject have compelled the works within this volume. We approach this challenge as mediators between a discipline that has traditionally been either distrustful or disinterested in the military (or both), and a defense community that has been misinformed or unaware of, or unconvinced of, anthropology's strengths of contributions to them.

Bifurcation within Anthropology

This introduction has focuses upon the relationship between the U.S. military and anthropologists, and has addressed the extent to which subject, audience, and voice inform a discussion of this relationship. Certainly the constraints and controls that these three elements pose for anthropologists is worthy of at least attention, if not concern, for those who choose to conduct ethnography among the military. However, another concern relates entirely to the anthropology community, which is generally bifurcated regarding the military. Some anthropologists speak negatively of the military from their position outside of the community and both disavow and decline opportunities to develop a relationship with the military; preserving distance is critical to these individuals, to whom proximity to the military may even be distasteful because they disagree vehemently with military missions or employment. Other anthropologists may criticize the military, but either do so from privileged positions inside military boundaries or do so constructively, aiming to change military doctrine or policy. This latter group generally distinguishes between the idea of the military as worthy of study and the employment of the military by the civilian leadership, of which they may or may not personally approve. In other words, these anthropologists separate their personal opinions of any particular military deployment or engagement from the inherent merit of the military as a research subject. Acknowledging this separation permits military anthropologists to study the military without feeling compelled to agree with any particular military employment. We assert that this work expands both understanding of the military as well as the usefulness of anthropology to the military, without compromising personal or professional standards.

Organization and Content of this Volume

This volume seeks to provide visions of and for U.S. military culture from a solid anthropological base. Understanding the U.S. military and the role it plays in the contemporary world order continues to be an important topic pursued by political scientists, sociologists, historians, and military policy analysts. The anthropologists who contribute to this volume are uniquely placed to engage the U.S. military from the inside. As a result, the volume articulates several important but relatively unknown cultural variations in the defense community through a variety of anthropological lenses. The military is, of course, an instrument of ultimate force. The stakes involved with understanding and helping to improve this institution are very high and tremendously important. The chapters in *The Anthropology of the Military* reflect significant directions of current research on the U.S. military. Essays in our book illustrate the unique contributions that anthropology can make to a holistic understanding of the military institution and to public policy regarding the military in the twenty-first century.

Robert Rubinstein points out that during the second half of the twentieth century, the study of the people and institutions that form the "military-industrial complex" was regarded largely with suspicion within anthropology. This distrust grew from many sources: In the 1960s anthropologists participated in counterinsurgency work in Southeast Asia, harming the people with whom they worked and the discipline itself. Development of weapons of mass destruction, and of more effective ways for deploying these arms, offended the basic commitments of many anthropologists. In the 1980s and 1990s anthropologists and others documented the ways in which militarism distorted society. In the popular media as well, portrayals of macho soldiers and heroic missilers crafted a stereotype of the military as both dangerous and politically homogeneous. Yet, like any social and cultural institution, the institutions and individuals in the military are heterogeneous. Contemporary militaries engage in a range of productive and defensive activities; no longer is "war-fighting" their sole mission. The U.S. military now engages in a variety of "operations other than war" including, for example, truce enforcement, delivery of humanitarian aid, and postconflict management of civil society. This wider scope of action, and the increasing involvement of military personnel in domestic politics, necessitates that the military participate in a broader range of policy discussions. Using data from the ethnographic study of U.S. peacekeepers, this chapter explores how the military accommodates a variety of political understandings, and how these political representations are developed, maintained, or transformed by service in peacekeeping units.

Jeanne Guillemin's work on the anthrax vaccination offers a unique perspective on the military based upon the contrast between individuals and institutions, centered around the anthrax vaccination debates. The Defense Department's December 1997 announcement of the universal anthrax vaccine inoculations program (AVIP) began an episode of new tension about acceptable medical risks associated with military service. The service men and -women who resisted the vaccinations numbered less than five hundred (virtually all were enlisted members). Yet their protest established a new link between potential combat-related illness (Agent Orange exposure and Gulf War Syndrome) and the potential side effects of preventive medical strategies. FDA approval of anthrax vaccine production lagged, while for four years the military courts firmly reinforced adherence to AVIP, which relied on limited existing stocks of the vaccine. Congressional hearings, which gave a forum to critics, further slowed the program and increased public skepticism. In the aftermath of the September–October 2001 anthrax attacks, groups of exposed civilians were offered the opportunity for anthrax vaccination but concern about the risks of side effects and scant scientific evidence for the vaccine's postexposure value made even government health officials unenthusiastic. By June 2002 the Pentagon, essentially abandoning AVIP, returned to its previous policy of selectively vaccinating soldiers liable to battlefield risks, for example, in the Middle East. This more restrained policy provoked no protest, although anthrax is by no means the only known biological weapon. Military protest of AVIP sprang from individualistic concerns about standardized medicine that were more common among enlisted members than officers. The protest raised important questions not simply about the protective value of vaccines against biological weapons, but about general counter-terrorism strategies and technologies for civilians.

Pamela Frese's chapter explores the multivocal concepts of "family" and "home" for fourteen retired officers' wives who are members of the "Golden Age" of the U.S. military culture. Their oral histories reflect the world view of other high ranking military and civilian members of an American aristocracy as they construct "family" and "home" as gendered domains of power and influence wherever members of the U.S. military were stationed. Incorporating more than biological and affinal relatives, a military officer's "family" includes fictive kin relationships that were established with members of various age-graded social institutions (military academies or elite Universities), and/or many philanthropic organizations. And finally, "family" also incorporates domestic/hired help as important kinds of fictive kin. Contemporary perspectives on gendered hegemonic structures might position white male officers at the top of a hierarchy under which their wives, enlisted men and their wives, and indigenous civilian personnel could be ranked. This generation of women, whose husbands were officers during World War II, Korea and Vietnam, envision the husband and wife as a team in which prescribed gender roles are distinctly different but equal spheres of influence. Based upon these women's views of the world, gender constructs continually redefine race and class relationships within an American aristocracy that includes the United States military of the "Golden Age."

Margaret Harrell explores gender roles and class among current Army spouses. She asserts that within the uniformed military, officer and enlisted communities are qualitatively and quantitatively separate, bounded groups. These groups are associated with many of the stereotypical characteristics of the civilian social classes. Consistent with stereotypes of the civilian lower class, junior enlisted personnel and their spouses are perceived to be young, immature, immoral, reproductively and financially irresponsible, and dirty and uncouth. This contrasts with the identity of officers, who are thought to portray maturity, moral virtue, family responsibility, and intelligence. There are extensive gender roles for Army spouses, but these roles vary dramatically for officer and enlisted spouses. This work explores the gender roles and how they differ by class, among Army spouses. Among the findings of this research are that enlisted spouses have negative experiences in the military community, and are generally isolated and voiceless, whereas officers' spouses play a very public and important role in the military community. Contrary to increased societal acceptance of working mothers and women in the workplace, the Army expectations for the spouses of certain officers—those commanding units—have actually increased in the 1990s. These expectations include extensive volunteerism and required entertaining and socializing generally incompatible with their own career interests. In addition, the performance of an officer's spouse performing these tasks is once again critical to an officer's success in the military.

Joshua Linford-Steinfeld relates how gender, weight control and physical readiness are major concerns of all U.S. Navy personnel. Ashore and on Navy ships, exercise options may be limited due to access and/or time issues, yet food is both abundant and a form of entertainment. Navy personnel who fail to meet body composition or physical fitness standards or have "eating disorders" may be denied promotions, may impede operational readiness, or may be administratively discharged. Research has shown that the Navy has the highest percentages of overweight personnel of any armed forces branch. This chapter utilizes an ethnographic methodology to investigate the relationship of weight control and physical readiness to: (1) discipline and regimentation (eating and exercise practices), (2) gender, and (3) "disordered" eating among Navy men.

Anna Simons links the military with anthropology when she considers the problems associated with "going native" for both anthropologists and military advisors. She argues that at first glance, it may be hard to imagine two sets of individuals more different in their approaches or their methods.

Yet, on closer examination, it turns out there are eerie parallels between the rapport that advisors need to build and the relationships that anthropologists try to cultivate. By examining the "going native" problem for advisors, this chapter will raise new questions for anthropologists. For instance, anthropologists' role has typically been far more passive than that of advisors. One might think that advisors would have an easier time being accepted by locals—Do they? Is "going native" even possible? And what dangers might be posed when advisors rightly or wrongly believe they have gone native. This chapter also examines the views taken by, and of, advisors in a series of settings usually thought of as anthropologists' turf: Saudi Arabia, Albania, Burma, the Vietnam highlands, and Afghanistan.

The chapters described above illustrate the relevance of anthropology to the military. Clementine Fujimura describes the institutional resistance by the Naval Academy to include anthropology among their academic offerings. She asserts that the modern military has traditionally pursued scientific development and technological innovation in the context of warfare superiority, and that the U.S. Naval Academy's curriculum reflects this philosophy by focusing on the so-called hard-sciences, such as engineering, thereby excluding subjects such as anthropology. This paper discusses attitudes traditionally held at the Naval Academy to course offerings in cultural studies and establishes that the lack thereof connotes a general lack of respect for such study as well as for cultural and individual diversity. However, today's military is faced with internal demographic changes and the need to not simply develop better weapons but to understand foreign societies at a deeper level. Admitting to these changes at home and abroad, the Naval Academy is slowly integrating more social science into its course work.

A Word about Our Authors

This book compiles works from a variety of authors with different backgrounds and expertise. One author, Robert Rubinstein, is an academic anthropologist whom the U.S. Army has sought for his contribution to their mission. Others are academic anthropologists who have embraced the military as targets of cultural richness. The civilian academic perspective is complemented by Anna Simons and Clementine Fujimura, who maintain their tie to anthropology as academics in military educational institutions. Margaret Harrell is employed at RAND, a nonprofit research organization which interacts with DoD on a daily basis, conducting research to support sound policy. Additionally, several of the authors grew up within or married into, military families. We believe this variation in professional and personal backgrounds contributes depth and variation to this volume.

Notes

*. The opinions expressed are solely the author's and do not represent those of RAND or any of its sponsors.
1. Some anthropologists prefer "contributor" and avoid the use of "informant" as they perceive it to harken back towards unpleasant memories of anthropologists being used against the best interest of indigenous people during the Vietnam era.
2. For example, one audience member at the 2002 AAAs asserted that if anthropologists interacted directly with the military, that anthropologists would have been responsible for the atrocities of the Nazis.

References Cited

Collins, Patricia Hill. 1995. "The Social Construction of Black Feminist Thought." In Nancy Tuana and Rosemarie Tong (eds.) *Feminism and Philosophy: Essential Readings in Theory, Reinterpretation, and Application.* Boulder, Colorado: Westview Press, Inc. Pp. 526–547.

CHAPTER 1

Peacekeepers and Politics: Experience and Political Representation Among U.S. Military Officers

Robert A. Rubinstein

Introduction

In May 2001 I received a call from a Marine Corps major that went something like this:

> Sir, we're interested in having a political anthropologist join us at a seminar later this month and you were recommended to us. The Marines have been involved in delivering humanitarian aid, and we've not done a very good job of it. But we know we're going to have to do it again. The situation we faced is that we bring humanitarian supplies to refugees. But the crowds are large and when the aid runs out they get unruly and turn on us. All we've been able to do in the past is use lethal force to protect ourselves. This meeting is to consider the cultural appropriateness of nonlethal weapons. It's no secret that we have been experimenting with directed energy and other nonlethal weapons. We know that using loud noises might disorient and knock people down. We're interested in knowing if using such a weapon in a Muslim crowd might cause problems—like if a man were to collapse on top of an unmarried women, would she then be ostracized? You know, things like that.

A couple of months later, I went to help train two Army units that were to be deployed in November as peacekeepers in Kosovo. This was the start of their preparations for that mission, and my colleague and I were working with the units on the negotiation skills they would need to call on as they carried out the myriad tasks to maintain order and civil society in their mission area. The hallways of the headquarters of the first unit with which we worked were festooned with memorabilia of various battles in which the unit had engaged and in which they had particularly distinguished themselves. The walls and display cases were filled with commendations, photographs, historical accounts—all testimony of effectiveness in war fighting.

Later that day, as we were conducting the "practical exercises" designed to give the members of the unit real problems to solve through negotiation, a young lieutenant said: "I'm not going to talk to this guy, I'll just tell him what to do. I've got all the weapons!"

In anthropology, the study of the people and institutions that form the "military-industrial complex" (or the defense community) has been regarded with suspicion. This distrust grew from many sources: In the 1960s anthropologists participated in counterinsurgency work in Southeast Asia, harming the people with whom they worked and the discipline itself. Development of weapons of mass destruction, the development of more effective ways for deploying these arms, and the well-documented ways in which militarism distorts societies all are contrary to anthropological commitments to advance the welfare of people, especially those with whom we work.

There is much anthropological literature critical of various aspects of the military-industrial complex (or the "security community," or the "military," or militarism). For the most part, this work focuses on the consequences of the acts of these people and institutions. In part because of our collective distrust of these institutions and people, little anthropological work engages them from the inside, as we would expect for any other domain of anthropological analysis.[1] Anthropology, for example, has no developed area like military sociology.

Encounters such as those I just described can serve to reinforce images of the defense community as hopelessly macho, obtuse, and one-dimensional in its responses to the world. This reinforces too the disciplinary bias against engaging in the study of these institutions. Yet in failing to treat the military and other components of the defense establishment as sites for serious ethnographic research, we fail ourselves. To members of defense communities, our critical commentaries often seem uninformed and unconnected to their reality; and thus the potential for anthropology to make a difference in that reality is diminished. It need not be that way, especially since serious ethnographic work with these communities reveals them to be sites of considerable variation and cultural generativity.

The day following the "I've got all the weapons" comment, my colleagues and I worked with the second unit. Although its headquarters was close to the first unit's, no more than half a mile down the road, the attitudinal distance between the two units was immense. The memorabilia that filled its walls and display cases were also commendations, photographs, and historical accounts. The theme of this unit's display was sacrifice in peace support operations. They celebrated its service in support of peacekeeping missions in Somalia, Bosnia, Haiti, and elsewhere. To be sure, the unit had no dearth of distinction in war-fighting in its history. Rather, it selected to honor and display its achievements in humanitarian efforts.

Culture, including organizational culture, is carried in a group's symbols and behavioral models (Hofstede 1991:9). The different displays at these two army units suggest that there is a great deal more heterogeneity in the defense community than anthropologists ordinarily suppose. When I began studying peacekeeping nearly twenty years ago, I too supposed that I would find a single military culture, and I suspected that this would work against the ends of peacekeeping. As my work progressed, I learned that these initial suppositions were quite wrong. In the following two sections I discuss first some dimensions of variation among military officers engaged in peacekeeping. Then I discuss some of the challenges that face anthropologists who wish to work with defense communities.

Cultural Variation in Peacekeeping

Military officers participating in peace support operations represent a variety of cultural groups. Not only do national militaries vary, but even within the militaries of a single nation peacekeepers come from different organizational cultures. These cultural differences affect the mission in many areas. How the operation is conducted, what the chances are for its success, and how personnel understand and are changed by the experience are all in part cultural. To illustrate this, I present some observations from my peacekeeping research. I draw only on materials from U.S. military officers, though my ethnographic work includes other nationalities as well.[2]

Motivation for Peacekeeping

Military officers come to peacekeeping for a variety of reasons and with a variety of understandings of the nature and value of such missions. Some of the officers sought out service in the United Nations Truce Supervision

Organization (UNTSO) for reasons consistent with the stereotyped view of the military. They thought it would provide a way to experience combat, or quasi-combat, and to gauge the effect that this would have on them.

> I had two great desires. One was to...be shot at to see what my reaction to being shot at was. The second goal was to work with foreign officers.
>
> —U.S. Army major

> As a Marine, you tend to look at that kind of a quasi-combat assignment. So I applied for it a couple of times, because...I would much rather have an Overseas Unaccompanied Assignment that was exciting, different, something new.
>
> —U.S. Marine lieutenant colonel

Others, however, sought service in UNTSO for other reasons, such as political education, personal growth, and career management.

> I wanted to come and visit this part of the world. It's a Holy Land tour that was very extensive and also not very expensive for me. It was something I always wanted to do, it's a scriptural thing to me.
>
> —U.S. Air Force major

> Coming to the end of my tour at Fort Ord, it was time for me to be transferred....I could not get a decent troop assignment again. So what I did was, a friend knew about this assignment and gave me the phone number about it and said: "You go to the Middle East for a year and than you go back to a troop post that you desire." So I called based on that. I wanted to go back to soldiers after this assignment.
>
> —U.S. Army major

> Yes, because we were already in Europe. There is a financial advantage for us, seven or eight hundred dollars a month, and the kids at university.
>
> —U.S. Air Force major

Just as officers came to UNTSO for diverse reasons, some linked to "doing manly things in a manly way," others to the micro-politics of military careers, and others still for highly personal motives, so too do officers on peacekeeping missions assimilate their experiences to different cultural models.

Experience and Political Development

It is an anthropological commonplace to note that culture helps shape how we experience the world and that it is through culture that that experience is made meaningful. The directive aspects of culture are what frame our expectations (d'Andrade 1984), and it is to those frames that our experience gets assimilated (Schön and Rein 1994). What officers expect of their service in peace operations and how they understand their experiences on those operations reflect organizational cultural differences (Rubinstein 2003). The two officers quoted next understand their mission in radically different terms: One sees the mission as a political project, the other as military one.

> Peacekeeping or not, it is a military organization. That might be the key word I would use.
>
> —U.S. Army major

> It's true that you feel a little insecure without a rifle in your hands, but the problem with having a rifle in your hands is that you tend to want to use it, maybe a little more than you should. I look at our mission to be as it were maintaining an international presence.
>
> —U.S. Marine major

And consider the differences evident in what the following two U.S. Army majors say they learned during their time as peacekeepers.

> You know, the realities are different when you're on the ground. Something else I learned here that I suspected, but didn't really know until I got over here, was Americans cannot begin to understand the Islamic mind at all. And that's very difficult.
>
> I came here I was neutral on the Israelis. Originally, way back, I was very pro-Israeli. When I finally got over here I was neutral on the Israelis.... Then I became very anti-Israeli. I knew nothing really about the Arabs, so I feel I've become more pro-Arab, so yes, I've changed on the Israelis, I've matured on the Arabs.

Perhaps some of these differences among peacekeepers are accentuated by individual proclivities. Yet the literature suggests that different groups within the military have systematic differences in worldview that relate to organizational culture (Ben-Ari 1998; Katz 1990; Pulliam 1997; Rubinstein 2003; Simons 1997; Winslow 1997). Anthropologists ought to describe and account for these variations, as they provide the points of entry through which we can affect change within those communities.

Challenges to the Anthropological Studies of the Defense Community

Anthropologists who wish to study defense communities face a number of challenges. Some of these derive from the nature of the phenomena. Others are challenges that are self-imposed by the discipline. Here I note three such challenges: access, money, and ethics.

Methodological Challenge of Studying Diffuse Communities: Access

Access is typically the first challenge that anthropologists face. Members of defense communities are used to scholars bothering them with questions. Therefore, there is a role to which an anthropologist seeking to do research among them can be assimilated. The challenge for anthropologists is that most of the researchers with whom the defense communities have had contact with have worked in traditions—such as survey research or international affairs analyses—that involve brief contacts between the researcher and the officers. Some of these researchers come from the staffs of politicians and are viewed with suspicion, as they have produced politically motivated reports that are unremittingly critical of the military and give, in the view of some, unfair portraits of the military. To some degree, anthropologists working in this area need to educate the defense community about ethnography. Once they have done this, the literature on studying these kinds of communities uniformly reports that access to them is much easier than anthropologists tend to assume.

In addition, the defense community challenges traditional ethnographic methods. Often the community is diverse and dispersed. Sometimes the individuals who make up these communities are more transient than ethnographers are used to engaging. These facts require methods that adapt traditional techniques to meet these challenges (Gusterson 1997; Rubinstein 1998a).

Disciplinary Obstacles: Funding

The ability to gain research funding is always critical to the conduct of ethnographic research. The standard sources of support for anthropological work are in principle open to supporting such work yet in practice closed to such studies.

To explore the question of funding, I looked at all of the grants that had been given between 1995 and 2001 by the National Science Foundation (NSF) to support cultural and linguistic anthropological research. I wanted to see first what proportion of these grants had been given to support work that looked at institutions of power in our own society—in Laura Nader's (1969) now classic term, projects that "studied up." More specifically, I wanted to know what proportion of these grants treated military or defense topics. The grants were reviewed by two raters who independently recorded their evaluation of each grant. Those about which there was disagreement were discussed, resulting in agreement on several grants. But because the numbers were so small, I report here as "studying up" or "military/defense" any grant for which at least one rater gave that score. If anything, this procedure will inflate the number of grants scored as "studying up" or "military/defense."[3]

In the seven years from 1995 through 2001, the National Science Foundation awarded just under $20 million to support cultural and linguistic anthropological research. This money was given to just over 400 research projects. Figures 1.1 and 1.2 show that during this seven-year period, just 3.53 percent of grants were made for projects that study up, and these accounted for only $691,751 of the nearly $20 million worth of grants made during the period.

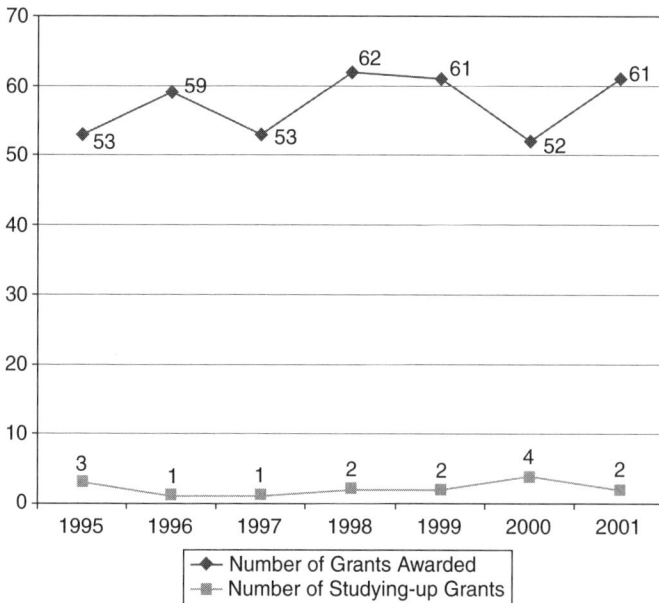

Figure 1.1 NSF Cultural and Linguistic Anthropology Awards, 1995–2001 Number of Grants Awarded: Studying-up versus Total Awards

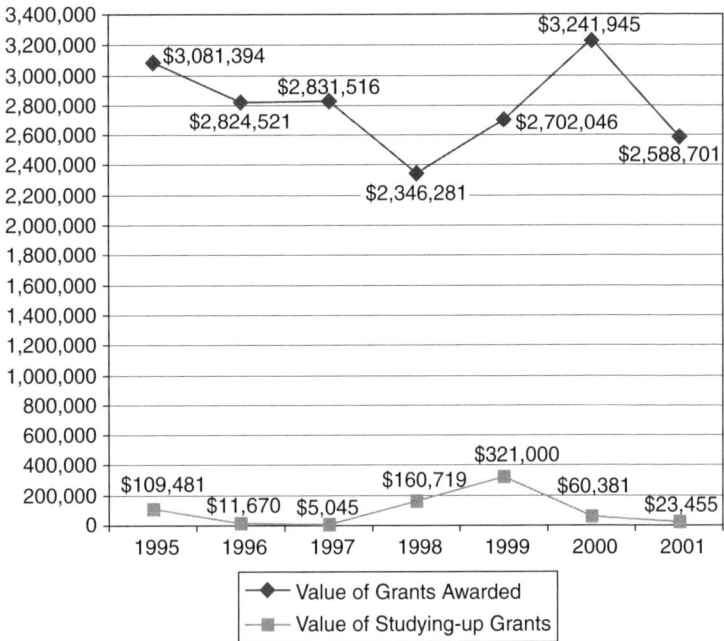

Figure 1.2 NSF Cultural and Linguistic Anthropology Awards, 1995–2001 Value of Grants Awarded: Studying-up Total Awards

The situation regarding support of anthropological research on topics relating to the military or defense is even starker. Figure 1.3 shows that between 1995 and 2001, only six grants were awarded to support research on military or defense topics.

These six grants received a total of $92,630, just one-half of 1 percent of all support given by the National Science Foundation for cultural and linguistic anthropological research during this seven-year period. Figure 1.4 displays the annual relationship of military/defense grants to all grants awarded.

Of course, the National Science Foundation is not the only source of funding for cultural and linguistic anthropological research. But there is little reason to suppose that the situation will be much different when other funders are considered.

During 1999 and 2000, the Wenner-Gren Foundation for Anthropological Research awarded just over $2.5 million to support cultural and

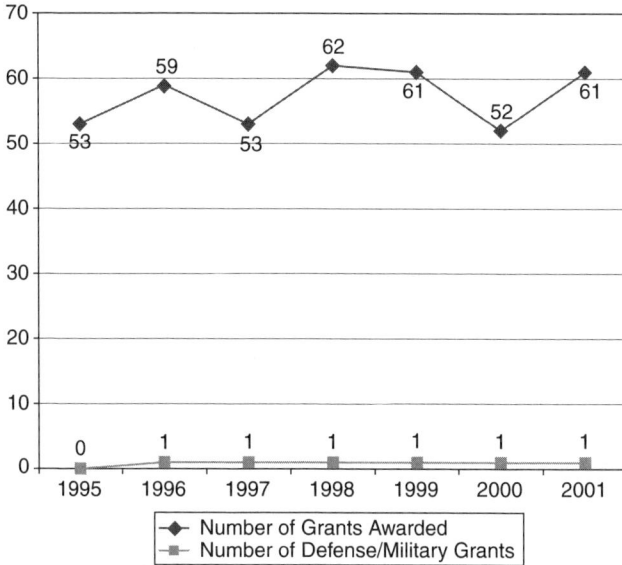

Figure 1.3 NSF Cultural and Linguistic Anthropology Awards, 1995–2001
Number of Grants Awarded: Military/Defense versus Total Awards

linguistic anthropological research. Of that sum, $32,075 was for projects relating to military and defense topics. As figure 1.5 shows, the number of grants relating to military or defense topics for these two years represents 1.25 percent of grants awarded.

What factors combine to create this picture are matters of speculation. In part, it seems to me that it is due to the enforcement of different standards for such work. For instance, since defense communities are powerful and regulated, researchers might be asked to demonstrate access in ways that go beyond that asked of scholars going into the field in a non-western country. Yet research permissions in the latter may in fact be more difficult to obtain than access to the defense community.

Ethics
Anthropologists who conduct ethnographic work within the defense community find themselves involved in the kinds of human exchanges that all anthropologists experience, whether their research takes them to a remote village or to the city. Such reciprocal exchanges must be managed so those social obligations are met while the integrity of the research and of the

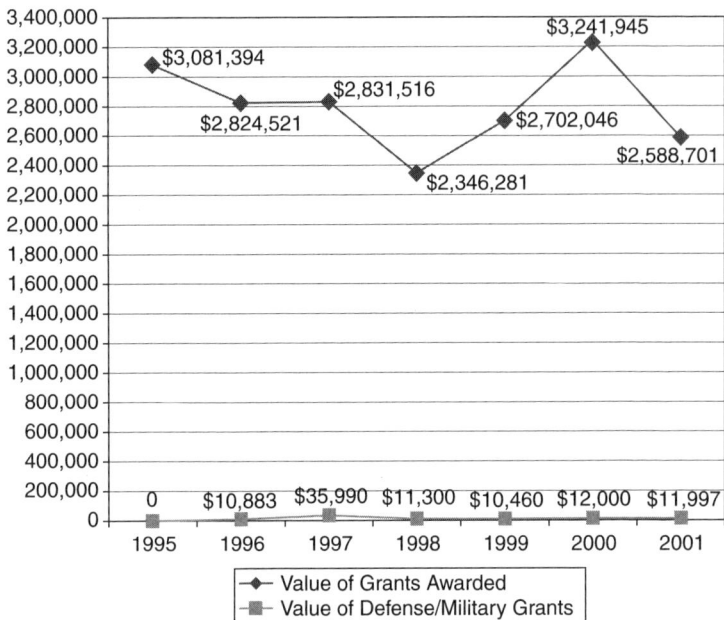

Figure 1.4 NSF Cultural and Linguistic Anthropology Awards, 1995–2001 Value of Grants Awarded: Military/Defense versus Total Awards

researcher are maintained. Because of the suspicion with which anthropologists view the defense community, researchers risk being stigmatized because of those exchanges.

Conclusion

Looking at the consequences of military and other defense community actions, anthropologists have correctly noted that, most frequently, they are detrimental to the communities with which we work. Arguably, one of the ways to effect a change in this circumstance is to change the way that the defense community does business. By identifying and understanding cultural variation within the defense community, anthropologists will find points of entry through which they can affect the actions and activities of defense communities.

Often the people we most need to affect with our work are members of communities that we stigmatize and avoid. The Central Intelligence Agency

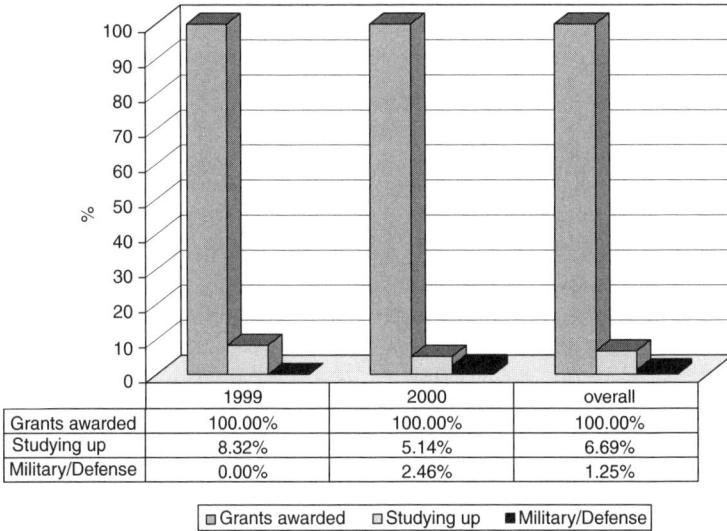

	1999	2000	overall
Grants awarded	100.00%	100.00%	100.00%
Studying up	8.32%	5.14%	6.69%
Military/Defense	0.00%	2.46%	1.25%

□ Grants awarded   □ Studying up   ■ Military/Defense

Figure 1.5 Wenner-Gren Foundation Cultural and Linguistic Anthropology Awards, 1999–2000 Value of Grants Made for Studying-up and for the Study of Military/Defense Topics as Percent of Total Awards

(CIA) and the military are just two examples. While there are historic reasons for this attitude among anthropologists, the voices from these communities have privileged places in discussions of contemporary affairs. As anthropologists, we will need to find professionally and ethically responsible ways to interact with them if we wish to make a real and meaningful difference in public policy.

Notes

1. There are some notable exceptions to this including (Ben-Ari 1998; Brasset 1997 [1988]; Gusterson 1996; Katz 1990; Pulliam 1997 [1988]; Simons 1997).
2. Examples are drawn from my fieldwork (Rubinstein 1989, 1993, 1998a,b, 2003). The principal site for this work was the United Nations Truce Supervision Organization, but it includes other missions as well. My work focuses on military officers. This research was supported by grants from the Wenner-Gren Foundation for Anthropological Research, the United States Institute of Peace, and the Ploughshares Fund. That support is gratefully acknowledged.

3. Examples of grants classified as studying-up and those classified as studying military or defense topics are:

Studying-Up

1995   Relational Business Contacts Between U.S. and Foreign Negotiators
1996   Ethnography of a Development Project
1997   Refugee Return-Resettlement and the Social Organization of Political Authority in Mozambique
1998   Worldview of Investment Banks
1998   Global Restructuring and Union Mobilization: An Analysis of Hotel Unionization in San Francisco, California
1999   Field Research on Violence and Healing: The International Construction of Knowledge about Treating Torture Survivors, Copenhagen and New York City
1999   The Reproduction of Knowledge for Regional Policies in the European Commission and Member-State Institutions, Italy, Spain, and Belgium
2000   Manufacturing Models for the Middle Class: Television and Influence in Indonesia
2001   Cultural Analysis of Risk Management in the Korean Venture Capital Industry
2001   Identity and Language in a Catalan Pediatric Unit
2001   Ethnographic Research on Market Culture and Global Free Trade Legislation in Dominica.

Military/Defense Grants

1997   Society and Military Practice in Sepik and Highland New Guinea
1998   Psychological Trauma and Post Traumatic Stress Disorder in Vietnam
1999   The Evolving Gender Roles of Military Spouses, Effects of a Changing Society
2000   Decolonization Activities on Guam at the Nexus of U.S. Colonialism and "Race"
2001   Ethnic Conflict in Guinea-Bissau, West Africa
2001   "The Nuclear Borderlands: The Legacy of the Manhattan Project in Post-Cold War New Mexico."

References Cited

Ben-Ari, Eyal. 1998. *Mastering Soldiers: Conflict, Emotions, and the Enemy in an Israeli Military Unit*. New York: Berghahn Books.

Brasset, Donna. 1997 [1988]. "Values and the Exercise of Power: Military Elites." In *The Social Dynamics of Peace and Conflict: Culture in International Security*. R. A. Rubinstein and M. L. Foster, eds. Pp. 81–90. Dubuque, IA: Kendall Hunt.

d'Andrade, Roy G. 1984. "Cultural Meaning Systems." In *Culture Theory. Essays on Mind, Self, and Emotion*. Richard Shweder and Robert Levin, eds. Pp. 88–119. Cambridge: Cambridge University Press.

Gusterson, Hugh. 1996. *Nuclear Rites: A Weapons Laboratory at the End of the Cold War*. Berkeley: University of California Press.

———. 1997. "Studying Up Revisited." *Political and Legal Anthropology Review*, 20:114–119.

Hofstede, Geert. 1991. *Cultures and Organizations: Software of the Mind*. New York: McGraw-Hill.

Katz, P. 1990. "Emotional Metaphors, Socialization and Roles of Drill Seargeants." *Ethos*, 18: 449–478.

Nader, Laura. 1969. "Up the Anthropologist—Perspectives Gained from Studying Up." In *Reinventing Anthropology*. D. Hymes, ed. Pp. 284–311. New York: Pantheon.

Pulliam, Linda. 1997 [1988]. "Achieving Social Competence in the Navy Community," In *The Social Dynamics of Peace and Conflict: Culture in International Security*. R. A. Rubinstein and M. L. Foster, eds. Pp. 91–106. Dubuque, IA: Kendall Hunt.

Rubinstein, R. A. 1989. "Culture, International Affairs and Peacekeeping: Confusing Process and Pattern." *Cultural Dynamics*, 2:41–61.

———. 1993. "Cultural Aspects of Peacekeeping: Notes on the Substance of Symbols." *Millennium: Journal of International Studies*, 22:547–562.

———. 1998a. "Methodological Challenges in the Ethnographic Study of Multilateral Peacekeeping." *Political and Legal Anthropology Review*, 21:138–149.

———. 1998b. "Peacekeeping Under Fire: Understanding the Social Construction of the Legitimacy of Multilateral Peacekeeping." *Human Peace*, 11:22–29.

———2003. "Cross-cultural Considerations in Complex Peacekeeping Operations." *Negotiation Journal*. 9 (1): 29–49.

Schön, Donald, and Martin Rein. 1994. *Frame Reflection. Toward the Resolution of Intractable Policy Controversies*. New York: Basic Books.

Simons, Anna. 1997. *The Company They Keep. Life Inside the U. S. Army Special Forces*. New York: Free Press.

Winslow, Donna. 1997. *The Canadian Airborne Regiment in Somalia: A Sociocultural Inquiry*. Ottawa, ON: Canadian Government Publishing.

CHAPTER 2

Medical Risks and the Volunteer Army

Jeanne Guillemin

T he field of anthropology is based on the study of traditional societies that, closely dependent on nature, were in constant danger of being overwhelmed by its destructive forces: storms, droughts, floods, and, above all, disease. As Bronislaw Malinowski argued in *Magic, Science and Religion* (1948), all humans rely on logic and experience to ward off serious danger. Yet, in modern societies, the medical technologies intended to reduce risks sometimes can be perceived as increasing it. The Pentagon's 1998 plan to protect all members of the military with an anthrax vaccine posed for some personnel what Mary Douglas (1992:83) calls "an insidious harm," an invisible contamination of the body severe enough to justify resisting government authority. The essential question the actions of these soldiers raised was whether military authorities could be trusted to protect them, not against death in battle but against the risks of bad medicine.

In late 1997, Secretary of Defense William Cohen alerted the nation to the dangers of the biological weapon anthrax and proposed a universal Anthrax Vaccine Immunization Program (AVIP) to vaccinate all 2.4 million military personnel. Four and a half years later, in June 2002, the administration of George W. Bush curtailed the program and returned to selective vaccination of troops headed for higher-threat areas. The short life of AVIP as a mandatory universal program highlighted the unusual health hazards apart from battle wounds and death for conventional munitions that soldiers should accept as part of their modern military service contract. Invisible, noiseless, often slow to take effect, biological weapons necessarily create fears of intentional, insidious, and lethal physical invasion from the very air we breathe (Balmer 1998; Guillemin 1999a). What then is the best defense? Is it another kind of bodily invasion, a relatively untested vaccine requiring six inoculations over the course of eighteen months?

Most soldiers complied with AVIP. But between 1998 and 2002, a small number of dissenters (around 450) refused the anthrax vaccination, of 500,000 who were inoculated at least once. Assisted by lawyers, physicians, and congressional advocates, the dissenters quickly made the public case that the safety and efficacy of the vaccine was questionable (Guillemin 1999b). Public dissent and controversy eventually improved government surveillance of adverse reactions to the vaccine, but other factors, such as lack of sufficient vaccine supplies, limited AVIP's goal of universal, total force, protection just as the United States embarked on an international "war against terrorism."

In 1998, the creation of AVIP extended an existing, largely unquestioned strategy for protecting soldiers against the new, ambiguous threat that anthrax posed to army bases, ships, and installations worldwide. During the 1991 Gulf War, out of concern that Iraq would use biological weapons, 150,000 soldiers were vaccinated against anthrax. Iraq had already used chemical weapons against its own Kurdish population and in the Iran–Iraq war. In 1993, the special United Nations task force (UNSCOM) formed under the 1991 cease-fire agreement discovered evidence in Iraq that Saddam Hussein had armed sixteen warheads with anthrax slurry and possessed anthrax bombs ready for use (Pearson 1999:143–150). In 1995, its relationship with Iraq unresolved and increasingly concerned about rogue nations, the United States began selectively vaccinating soldiers for active duty in Southwest Asia and near North Korea, which was also suspected of having biological weapons. President Clinton himself, influenced by expert scientists, was convinced that biological weapons represented the most serious threat to American security and that vaccines were an important national defense (Miller et al. 2001:223–244).

AVIP was planned in phases, proceeding from those deployed in the most dangerous parts of the world to those at moderate and, finally, at minimal risk. Phase I of AVIP was planned to begin in July–August 1998, Phase II in late 1999, and Phase III in 2001. Shortly after the AVIP decision, Iraq evicted UNSCOM inspectors. In March 1998, envisioning the mobilization of 200,000 soldiers, the Pentagon jump-started the first phase of AVIP and began the inoculation of 36,000 military personnel already in Southwest Asia.

The Guinea Pig Soldier

Writing in the nineteenth century, Georg Simmel observed that military and religious institutions are alike in that they claim the individual wholly (Simmel 1950:359). The context for protest against AVIP was a questioning of just how complete military authority should be; that is, had the military the right to take risks with soldiers' health that could cause long-term harm?

Beginning with the 1978 congressional review of 1950s radiation exposure, historic instances of military disregard for the risks of toxic exposures followed one after another. Like prison and asylum inmates, soldiers once seemed exempt from even rudimentary ethical concerns about the medical hazards of tests and experiments. Looked at another way, members of the modern volunteer peacetime army had developed individualistic expectations, including a long, postservice civilian life.

The impetus for investigating the past often came from veterans, advocates, and Congress. Atomic bomb testing in the 1950s was the first major revelation about the heedless exposure of enlisted men at test sites. From 1966 to 1972, the U.S. offensive biological weapons program, Project Whitecoat, recruited conscientious objectors among Jehovah's Witnesses in open-air experiments with brucellosis. In the 1960s, Project SHAD (Shipboard Hazard and Defense) exposed Navy, Marine, and Army personnel to dozens of toxic biological releases. At the same time, from 1950 to 1970, U.S. military experiments exposed hundreds of military volunteers to lewisite and mustard gas with no explanation of possible consequences and without follow-up treatment (Institute of Medicine 1993).

As the field of medical ethics emerged in the 1970s, civilians became protected from experimentalism by human subjects' guidelines and laws. The worst instances of using soldiers as guinea pigs also seemed in the past. Yet with the Vietnam War, experiments on the battlefield with new toxic substances emerged as a new order of risk. Less compliant and less trusting than the older generation, veterans soon voiced their suspicions. The claims of Vietnam veterans in the 1980s that Agent Orange had damaged their health and caused birth defects in their children were followed by years of investigation and reports, none definitive. The Pentagon response was basically a reluctance to take responsibility.

In the 1990s, the claims of Gulf War veterans that a combination of toxins had made them sick met similar reluctance, generating detailed investigation but little causal evidence and much disagreement among experts (Cotton 1994). Yet historically Gulf War claimants made the most pressing demands to date for the military to take responsibility for veterans' ambiguous, lifelong maladies from battlefield toxins. At the radical fringe, Gulf War veterans also expressed deep distrust of the military and federal government, using the Internet to present conspiracy theories (Fortun 1999). At the same time, the scientific investigation of the Gulf War Syndrome, which the government admitted existed, continued. For example, in October 1999, while the controversy about AVIP was at its height, RAND released a report, funded by the Department of Defense, speculating that pyridostigmine bromide, used during the Gulf War against possible Iraqi chemical attack, could cause serious nerve damage in hot, stressful conditions (Golomb 1999).

With the announcement of the AVIP initiative, the anthrax vaccinations of many Gulf War Syndrome sufferers came to the fore as a prime suspect for their symptoms and a warning to younger soldiers not to trust the Pentagon with their health. A sense of identification with the issues of Gulf War veterans permeated resistance to AVIP. A New York state parent protesting on behalf of a Marine son told the Associated Press: "It's morally wrong. They are using our children as guinea pigs. We are not at war. . . . This is something that could be delayed until further tests are done." The same parent pointed to fears of lifelong sickness—fatigue, headaches, dizziness, lupus, cancer, infertility, and birth defects—often associated with Gulf War Syndrome (AP 1999).

Efficacy

U.S. soldiers on active duty are routinely vaccinated against exotic diseases. But as critics were quick to point out in early 1998, the anthrax vaccine was different. Relative to others, it lacked a history of both safety and efficacy, although the disease itself dates back to the origins of pastoral societies. An ancient disease of grazing animals, anthrax is caused by a bacterium, Bacillus anthracis, which kills its host in order to escape in spore form to the soil, where dormant it awaits another grazing animal. Until the 1860s, when Louis Pasteur invented the first animal vaccine, humans were vulnerable to gastrointestinal anthrax from eating infected meat, or to cutaneous or inhalational anthrax from contact with contaminated animal products. Successful and routine inoculations of herds worldwide made anthrax an unusual disease, with two exceptions. One was the emergence of cutaneous and, more rarely, inhalational anthrax in industrial settings, especially textile mills and tanneries, from infected hides, hair, and wool. The other was the development of anthrax spores as a biological weapon, in aerosol form, by major world powers.

The vaccine used in the AVIP effort had its origins in the U.S. offensive biological weapons program. Its main drawback was that it had never been tested on humans as a means of preventing inhalational anthrax and, for ethical reasons, it could not be (Sidel, Nass, and Ensign 1998). In the 1950s, several American mills were sites for vaccine experiments involving control groups and the use of placebos. The vaccine seemed to reduce cutaneous cases; inhalational cases seemed never to happen. Then, in 1957, at a mill in Manchester, New Hampshire, five unvaccinated workers (two on placebos) contracted inhalational anthrax from contaminated Indian goat hair (Brachman et al. 1960). Four of these workers died, but these few cases proved little about the vaccine's protective value for other exposed workers.

In 1970 AVA (Anthrax Vaccine Adsorbed) was licensed by the Food and Drug Administration (FDA). Unlike the live vaccines used in Russia and China, it is noncellular. Its basic mechanism is the subcutaneous introduction of one of the three anthrax proteins, PA (Protective Antigen), which, with the help of aluminum hydroxide, stimulates antibodies (Brachman and Friedlander 1994; Dixon, Meselson, Guillemin, and Hanna 1999).

There was also a question about the vaccine's potency. Six inoculations over an eighteen-month period seemed to produce full immunity; even three shots seemed to convey nearly complete resistance. But these estimates were based on conjecture about observable levels of antibodies detectable after each inoculation. Did high antibody levels mean greater immunity against inhalational anthrax? The answer was a probable but not a certain yes.

A U.S. Army study of sixty-eight rhesus monkeys, quickly completed in1990, just prior to the Gulf War, suggested that the vaccine had a post-exposure value in preventing inhalational anthrax, especially if combined with antibiotics (Friedlander et al. 1993). Still, compared to the enormous amount of information on vaccines against more common infectious diseases, AVA remained a relative unknown.

In March 1998, as troops in Southwest Asia were being vaccinated, a new controversy about the vaccine's efficacy emerged: that it might not protect against new strains of anthrax. Research done by Russian scientists and presented at a British conference showed that genetic manipulation could produce an anthrax strain resistant to the live Soviet vaccine (Pomerantsev et al. 1995). Other research indicated that the anthrax in the 1979 Sverdlovsk epidemic, accidentally released from a Soviet military facility, was composed of multiple strains (Jackson et al. 1997). Would new or mixed strains developed by U.S. enemies prove resistant to the U.S. vaccine? In a press interview, the Army Surgeon General, Ronald Blanck, downplayed the dangers of such futuristic possibilities, saying: "Our vaccine protects, as near as we know, against all of these strains because the vaccine is against a part of the bacteria [PA] that doesn't change, that doesn't define one strain from another" (Reuters 1998).

A serious problem loomed behind this exchange: a range of biological weapons—tularemia, plague, and smallpox among them—had been developed by the United States and the Soviet Union. NATO (North Atlantic Treaty Organization) and the World Health Organization listed around thirty such weapons. Would the anthrax vaccine or any other vaccine or medical intervention be capable of providing the immunological shield necessary against these threats? Despite military disclaimers, new biotechnologies could amplify the capacity of biological weapons to disable or kill. Not just the Pentagon but the White House and the federal government in general were focused on short-term defenses against the possible use of biological weapons by hostile nations and terrorists.

Safety, Risk, and Manufacturing Standards

Three main safety issues troubled the AVIP effort. The first had to do with quality of the vaccine. The FDA had issued a report in February 1998 faulting the facility that had manufactured the vaccine, the Michigan Biologic Products Institute (MBPI), on its chronic failure to meet production standards. Meryl Nass, a general practitioner in Maine and an advocate for dissenting soldiers, obtained a copy of the report and circulated her summary of it to colleagues. In brief, the MBPI failed to test or review its production procedures, to monitor expiration dates or labeling, to test stability or sterility, to write down operating procedures, or to make sure lots that failed testing were not used. The variability of quality in lots was especially troubling, although Secretary of Defense Cohen promised that every lot would be tested before shipment.

Earlier, in January 1998, Nass circulated the conclusions of scientist Peter Turnbull, a United Kingdom government anthrax expert, after his review of experiments with guinea pigs using the Michigan vaccine. He found that the U.S. vaccine offered only erratic protection and added that "the injection into human beings of crude and undefined preparations is increasingly regarded as unsatisfactory, particularly, as in the case of the anthrax vaccines, when they are associated with frequent complaints of unpleasant side-reactions" (Turnbull 1991:539).

Nass also turned to two 1994 sources. One was a report of the Senate Committee on Veterans' Affairs, which drew this conclusion: "Although anthrax vaccine had been considered approved prior to the Persian Gulf War, it was rarely used. Its safety, particularly when given to thousands of soldiers in conjunction with other vaccines, is not well established" (U.S. Senate

1994:197). The report went on to suggest that the anthrax vaccine may be related to Gulf War Syndrome, although subsequent studies were unable to establish this connection. The second source was an article from a textbook by two eminent anthrax experts, the U.S. Army's Arthur Friedlander and retired Centers for Disease Control scientist Philip Brachman. That article presented several reasons why the anthrax vaccine was unsatisfactory. The lack of standardization, questions about potency and purity, the undefined nature of the vaccine and the presence of constituents that may be undesirable—were clear calls for a new and better vaccine (Brachman and Friedlander 1994). These criticisms undermined the Pentagon's assertion that the vaccine was safe.

In July 1998 a new private company, Bioport, bought MBPI and, with several million dollars in federal support, proceeded to construct a larger facility to meet the projected demands of AVIP. Headed by retired Admiral William Crowe, former head of the Joint Chiefs of Staff, Bioport quickly ran afoul of the FDA, again on the issue of production and quality standards. The military had to rely on old MBPI lots of vaccine, which caused it some embarrassment. At a December 13, 1998 press conference, Pentagon officials put the best spin on anthrax vaccine stocks but had to admit that one million doses of some two million available were probably unsuitable for use and that Phase II of AVIP would necessarily be delayed (Federal News Service 1998).

Along with downplaying adverse reactions, the Pentagon had a policy of not tallying incidents of dissent or attrition caused by fear of the anthrax vaccine. Throughout 1999, though, a combination of court cases, resignations by reserve pilots, media coverage, and congressional hearings made it impossible for military leaders to ignore critics.

Two entrepreneurial Washington lawyers, Todd Ensign of Citizen Soldier and Mark Zaid of The James Madison Project, took the lead in promoting legal redress for dissenters. In April 1998, Zaid was the first lawyer to represent military dissenters—three sailors on the U.S.S. Independence. By the end of 1998, several dozen sailors and soldiers had been disciplined for refusing the vaccine.

The rumors of dizziness and memory loss associated with the vaccine made reserve pilots especially wary. Those employed by private airlines had to pass regular physicals; being anything less than fit could mean the loss of their jobs. In December 1998–January 1999, nine pilots resigned from the Connecticut Air National Guard and became the first reserve officers to reject AVIP. One of them, Dom Possemato, told the media: "I'm willing to let the Iraqis take a potshot at me and put me in my grave. I'm not willing to let my country do that." Two airmen in the Pennsylvania National Guard also resigned rather than be vaccinated; more would follow. A young airman at Travis Air Force Base in California, Jeff Bettendorf, made the news for not only refusing to be vaccinated but, with Zaid's counsel, for requesting a full court-martial hearing. At this time, in early 1999, according to the Pentagon, 166,000 soldiers had received at least the first AVA inoculation.

Ensign, Nass, and other activists organized town meetings near military bases around the country, in San Diego, upstate New York, and Arlington, Virginia, to encourage dissenters to speak. Meanwhile, activists and dissenters secured the attention of about a dozen members of Congress, which set in process hearings, legislation, and investigations and reviews by the General Accounting Office, the Centers for Disease Control, the National Research Council, and the Institute of Medicine (IOM) at the National Academy of Sciences. In early May, the General Accounting Office reported its findings—that its committee could not determine if AVA was safe or effective—to a hearing of the House Subcommittee concerned with veterans' affairs, chaired by Republican Christopher Shays of Connecticut.

At this juncture, the Pentagon admitted that around two hundred military personnel had either resigned or been disciplined for refusing the vaccine, but also pointed out that 223,000 had received at least one inoculation.

A persistent problem with AVIP was that the military failed to convince at least some military personnel that anthrax was a lethal battlefield threat, worth the possible long-term risks of the vaccine. Iraq had not used either chemical or biological weapons during the Gulf War; the promise of annihilating retribution from the United States and its allies had probably been the deterrent. Protective face masks and suits and postexposure antibiotics, effective against a range of biological weapons, were available alternatives to the vaccine. The resumption of armed conflict in the Middle East was uncertain. In addition, key allies were not requiring their soldiers deployed in Southwest Asia to submit to anthrax vaccines. The United Kingdom left its program voluntary and experienced some loss of face when, in June 1998, an entire battleship crew refused the vaccine out of fear of contracting Gulf War Syndrome. The French saw no value in an anthrax vaccination program or in resumed conflict with Iraq. Meanwhile, the American press was reporting incidents in which soldiers were told they had to consent to the anthrax vaccinations or Military Police would hold them down while the inoculation was forced on them.

Immediate and Long-term Adverse Reactions

The tendency of military leaders to discourage full reporting of adverse reactions made critics suspicious of all Pentagon evidence about the vaccine's side effects. Congress later noted the problem of underreporting and, in November 1999, required the Pentagon to begin nonmilitary reviews of AVIP, which it did, in conjunction with the National Research Council and the Institute of Medicine. Even so, statistics on side effects were open to interpretation. From the Pentagon's perspective, a certain percentage and range of immediate adverse reactions were normal. In a March 10, 1998 press release aimed at military personnel, the Pentagon noted that "[a]s with other vaccinations, pain may occur at the site of injection. Temporary side effects (sore arm, redness, and slight swelling) may occur." The factual basis for this restrained description was slim. For thirty years, various vaccinated workers at Fort Detrick had self-reported reactions at rates that hovered around 2 percent for "local events," at the site of the inoculation, with no serious events ever reported. Studies in 1992 and 1994 of booster shots given to 495 men vaccinated for the Gulf War reported that 27 percent experienced "mild reactions," 4.7 percent, "moderate," and none "severe" (IOM 2002:92–93).

Studies conducted in 1998 and 1999 on newly vaccinated men and women showed a somewhat different picture. In a retrospective report through questionnaires of 2,824 U.S. military personnel in Korea (2,214 men and 610 women), nearly 40 percent of the men and 68 percent of the women reported local events. In addition, 1.1 percent of the men and 4.1 percent of the women reported severe reactions categorized as pain, itching, or a subcutaneous lump. The greater sensitivity of women to the inoculation, not unusual with vaccinations, was later shown in other studies (IOM 2002: 92–105).

The military also normalized the vaccine by comparing it to DTP (diptheria tetanus pertussis) childhood vaccinations, for which there is a known one in one thousand chance of serious, even fatal complications, and to the more serious temporary reactions to whooping cough and typhoid shots. Nothing known about the anthrax vaccine indicated a side effect so dire as death. When two suspicious deaths were reported, the Pentagon, relying on autopsy data, declared them unrelated to the vaccine and was supported in this by other government reviewers (IOM, 2002:9).

In its March 10, 1998 press release and in other communications, the Pentagon emphasized that the vaccine had been in use since 1970 with no known long-term consequences. In truth, no effort had been made to track long-term side effects among the relatively few civilians (veterinarians, laboratory workers, mill workers, and livestock handlers) or military personnel vaccinated before 1991 and the Gulf War. No information existed on women's reactions. And the records of the Gulf War inoculations of 150,000 soldiers had been lost or were incomplete. Facts that might have reduced dissent—or increased it—did not exist.

From the soldiers' perspectives, as far as they were known, troubling side effects that seemed more than temporary included dizziness, nausea, persistent subcutaneous lumps, and memory loss. While the Pentagon was thinking in terms of battle-ready troops, some, perhaps many, soldiers were intimately engaged in calculating medical contingencies in a risk-obsessed culture (Giddens 1991:99–108).

An important consequence of the soldiers' dissent was the outside review of studies related to adverse reactions to AVA summarized in the 2002 Institute of Medicine's special committee report. The IOM report refers often to the surveillance system called VAERS (Vaccine Adverse Event Reporting System), established in 1990 and run jointly by the Centers for Disease Control and the Food and Drug Administration. Vaccine recipients and their families are free to submit reports, although most reports come from healthcare providers and manufacturers constructing standard evidence for vaccine trials. The report faulted the Department of Defense for limiting VAERS reports of anthrax vaccine reactions to only related hospitalization, time lost from duty that exceeded twenty-four hours, or unusual or severe reactions. The IOM report also noted that the option of reporting to VAERS was unknown to some military physicians and to most soldiers and reservists surveyed by the General Accounting Office (GAO 2000). The IOM committee reviewed VAERS data on AVA going back to 1990. Of 1,623 reports, only 57 involved hospitalization and 161 involved more than twenty-four hours lost duty time. At least 10 of the 57 hospitalizations seemed directly due to the side effects of the vaccine. Eighty-nine of the 161 "duty loss incidents" were judged likely to have been directly caused by the vaccine.

Not only underreporting but a lack of information on denominators (how many soldiers in total were vaccinated, where and when and from what lots) undermined the AVIP VAERS figures. The failure, as the IOM (2002:80–81) noted, lay with the Department of Defense, which was keeping complete records of AVIP but not linking them to VAERS or other reports.

Did the anthrax vaccine cause serious health risks? The IOM and a vaccine review committee formed by the Department of Health and Human Services in 1998 both dismissed five cases of Guillain-Barré syndrome and one case of diabetes, along with other serious conditions, as side effects of the vaccine (IOM 2002:86–87). In reviewing additional studies, the IOM committee concluded: "There is no evidence that life-threatening or permanently disabling immediate-onset adverse events occur at higher rates in individuals who have received AVA than in the general population" (2002:128). The Pentagon interpreted this conclusion as a vote of confidence and advertised the report on its website (www.anthrax.osol.mil).

After four years, only 69,000 soldiers had received the full six anthrax vaccine inoculations. Many soldiers received only one or two shots. But the consequences were unclear.

The Reevaluation of Risk

In January 2000 the Pentagon put the private company Battelle on contract for $1.5 million a year to help Bioport resolve quality control problems. By July, dissenters were less of a problem for AVIP than Bioport's persistent inability to obtain FDA certification. The Department of Defense announced that it was limiting vaccination to personnel in the Persian Gulf and Korean peninsula areas, that is, it was stuck in Phase I. In late November, the Pentagon announced that this restricted policy would continue. Aside from an emergency stockpile, only 60,000 doses of AVA remained.

The promise of universal vaccination depended on having adequate stores of some vaccine, either AVA or an improved version. But Bioport's failure to meet FDA standards persisted. There might be enough of the old AVA to transition slowly into Phase II, but Phase III, the inoculation of military personnel at low risk of deployment to overseas hot spots, was nowhere in sight.

Rather than diminishing in importance, defensive responses to the threat of biological weapons received as much attention in the Bush administration as they had in the Clinton administration. Anthrax lost some of its primacy as a biological weapons threat to smallpox, which the United States and the Soviets had developed as a weapon. Although this contagious disease had been eradicated from the world since 1980, some experts suspected that terrorists might have access to secret reserves or to the legitimate reserves safeguarded by Russia and the United States. The vulnerability of American civilians was a central issue, resulting in large-scale plans for emergency smallpox vaccine stockpiles and vaccination of first responders. Iraq continued to resist United Nations inspections, but seemed to pose no immediate threat to the region. The September 11 terrorist attacks on the United States, followed shortly by the anthrax postal attacks, moved the nation into a wartime alert that precluded dissent, within or outside the military. The anthrax letters, far from the citywide attacks on which federal bioterrorism response plans were based, nonetheless renewed anxieties about the vulnerability of American soldiers and civilians to inhalational anthrax. An anonymous perpetrator sent at least four and perhaps as many as seven letters containing anthrax spores to American media offices and to two members of the U.S. Senate (World Health Organization 2003). Phrases in four recovered letters, such as "Death to Israel" and "Praise to Allah," made it appear at first that Middle Eastern Islamic fundamentalists might be responsible. Analyses by Federal Bureau of Investigation linguistic and handwriting experts and the processed anthrax powder itself suggested instead an American weapons scientist, whose aim might have been to impress the nation with the danger of anthrax.

The main medical lesson from the anthrax attacks was that quick recognition of pathogenic anthrax and rapid post-exposure prophylaxis prevented death and illness. On October 15, around forty Senate employees were exposed to tens of thousands of anthrax spores emitted from an envelope sent to Senate Democratic Majority Leader Tom Daschle. Capitol Hill police did a fast, accurate assay of the powder, and emergency medical personnel dispensed antibiotics to those exposed, none of whom fell ill. This same tactic of "test and treat" was used after the discovery of unpredicted, extensive postal contamination. Eight of the eleven inhalational anthrax cases were among postal or mailroom workers, for whom the danger of spore dispersal from unopened letters were unknown or, in the later cases, discounted by public health officials. Six of the inhalational victims survived, much better than the 80 to 90 percent anticipated death rate. Anthrax suddenly seemed manageable.

Did the anthrax vaccine have any of the post-exposure defensive value of antibiotics? Data from the 1979 Sverdlovsk epidemic had already shown that the dormant anthrax spores could remain in the lungs as long as forty-three days after exposure and then, germinating in the lymph nodes, cause illness and death (Guillemin 1999a:236; Meselson et al. 1994). U.S. Army monkey experiments suggested an even longer dormancy period, up to sixty or a hundred days. More than 30,000 people were prescribed either ciprofloxacine or doxycyline for as long as sixty days—to kill anthrax bacteria before they produced deadly toxins. Thousands of civilians were given the option of receiving the military's AVA as their thirty to sixty days of antibiotics ended. Government health officials were publicly ambivalent, especially about the sparse post-exposure data from a single study (Friedlander 1993).

In the months following the anthrax postal attacks, the Pentagon struggled with its vaccine schedule until on June 28, the Bush administration announced the Clinton AVIP policy would end. From then on, only military personnel expected to spend fifteen days or more in high-risk areas overseas (Iraq and other Persian Gulf countries, the Korean peninsula, and possibly Afghanistan) would be vaccinated against anthrax. This effort (actually Phase I) would require a third of the U.S. vaccine supply. Another third of the vaccine supply would be for other government departments, such as State and Justice, whose employees might be under threat, and government-paid contractors working on anthrax defenses.

The more surprising Bush administration announcement was that, as insurance against domestic bioterrorism, another third of the vaccine supply would go to civilian stockpiles to be stored by the Department of Health and Human Services in secret warehouses throughout the country. These stockpiles would be for postexposure use following a catastrophic attack. All the data justifying the relative safety for this civilian strategy were from the military. In the months prior to this announcement, the government had fifteen articles on AVIP published or in press. Like the IOM report, these reports minimized serious side effects. A diverse civilian population—including children, the elderly, the malnourished, the sick, and greater numbers of women—would be at predictably higher risk than healthy, predominantly male troops. But in a true catastrophe, one or two inoculations might reduce risks of infection and death. Or so government officials presumed.

The decision to end universal vaccination was driven in part by the diminished availability of AVA. Officials remained vague about just how many doses of vaccine the government had in stock, employing the phrase "a constrained supply situation." Still, future demands for the vaccine were obvious. With Iraq a target in the Bush administration's war against terrorism, the Pentagon estimated that 200,000 soldiers might be deployed to the Persian Gulf. The military would need more than one million doses to vaccinate them fully. As an alternative, with current stocks, soldiers could receive just three inoculations and probably be 90-percent protected. The Pentagon affirmed that it wanted to buy three million doses over the next three years. It would rely on Bioport, which finally, in January 2002, had met FDA criteria, and also encourage competition from other companies and universities.

In the fall of 2002, mobilization for war in Iraq quelled dissent and deferred hard questions bout the anthrax vaccine risks. Over 500,000 enlisted and reserve soldiers had received at least one anthrax inoculation.

Conclusion

"The body is our most intimate cosmos," Yi-Fu Tuan (1979: 87), writing on disease, reminds us, "a system whose harmony is felt rather than merely perceived with the mind. Threaten the body, and our whole being revolts." Unlike Agent Orange or the Gulf War Syndrome, the threat of the anthrax vaccine was a specific bodily invasion that dissenters feared would cause chronic illness. The vaccine's efficacy against a biological weapon—since it remained untested on humans—was less a source of anxiety than its capacity to permanently sicken soldiers. Yet the decision to stockpile AVA for civilian use never would have been made if strong evidence for adverse effects had been reported and legitimated by experts. Previous generations of Agent Orange and Gulf War Syndrome veterans felt they had been used as guinea pigs in battlefield experiments that essentially failed and would not be repeated. In contrast, soldiers vaccinated during the AVIP program were test cases for other soldiers and, importantly, for civilians who, lacking masks and suits, would be especially vulnerable during an anthrax aerosol attack. Still, doubts must remain about whether the military calculation of medical risks in battle can ever translate to valid research science or to the secure protection of civilians.

In future years, the hundreds of thousands of anthrax-vaccinated American soldiers, no matter how stoically they accepted the old-stock anthrax inoculations, are bound to wonder whether they bear some undefined health burden—if, for example, their immune systems were permanently damaged by compulsory vaccination (Martin 1994:198). Some percentage of them may well demand legal proof that they were not recklessly exposed to long-term health hazards. The Pentagon resented AVIP critics but may be grateful later for the better surveillance, record keeping, and science-based proof they demanded, and wish it had done more.

References Cited

Associated Press (AP). 1999. "Families of Two Marines Protest Imposed Anthrax Vaccinations." January 25.

Balmer, Brian. 1998. "Using the Population Body to Protect the National Body: Germ Warfare Tests in the UK After WW II." In *Proceedings of the "Using Bodies" Conference*, Pp. 3–4. London: Wellcome Institute for the History of Medicine. September.

Brachman, Philip S., Stanley L. Plotkin, Forrest H. Bumford, and Mary M. Atchison. 1960. "An Epidemic of Inhalation Anthrax: The first in the Twentieth Century." *American Journal of Hygiene*, 72(3):3–9.

Brachman, Philip S., and Arthur M. Friedlander. 1994. "Anthrax." In *Vaccines*, Stanley A. Plotkin and Edward A. Mortimer, eds. Pp. 729–739. Philadelphia: W.B. Saunders.

Cotton, Paul. 1994. "Veterans Seeking Answers to Syndrome Suspect They were Goats in Gulf War." *Journal of the American Medical Association*, 27(20):1559–1561.

Dixon, Terry C., Matthew Meselson, Jeanne Guillemin, and Philip C. Hanna. 1999. "Anthrax. Bacillus Anthracis Infection Revisited." *New England Journal of Medicine*, 345(11):815–825.

Douglas, Mary. 1992. "Witchcraft and Leprosy." In *Risk and Blame. Essays in Cultural Theory.* Pp. 83–101. London: Routledge.

Federal News Service. 1998. "Special Defense Briefing: The Anthrax Vaccination and Inoculation Program." December 13.

Fortun, Kim. 1999. "Lone Gunmen: Legacies of the Gulf War, Illness, and Unseen Enemies." *Paranoia Within Reason: A Casebook on Conspiracy as Explanation.* In George E. Marcus, ed. Pp. 343–374. Chicago: University of Chicago Press.

Friedlander, Arthur M., S. L. Welkos, M. L. Pitt, J. W. Ezzell et al. 1993. "Postexposure Prophylaxis against Experimental Inhalational Anthrax." *Journal of Infectious Diseases* 167(5):691–702.

General Accounting Office (GAO). 2000. "Anthrax Vaccine. Preliminary Results of GAO's Survey of Guard/Reserve Pilots and Aircrew Members." GAO-01-92T. Washington, D.C.: General Accounting Office.

Giddens, Anthony. 1991. *Modernity and Self-Identity: Self and Society in the Late Modern Age.* Stanford, CA: Stanford University Press.

Golomb, Beatrice A. 1999. *A Review of the Scientific Literature as it Pertains to Illnesses of Gulf War Veterans, Vol. II: Pyridostigmine Bromide.* MR-1018/2-OSD. Santa Monica, CA: RAND.

Guillemin, Jeanne.1999a. *Anthrax: The Investigation of a Deadly Outbreak.* Berkeley, CA: University of California Press.

———. 1999b. "Soldiers, Rights and Medical Risks: The Protest Against Universal Anthrax Vaccinations." *Human Rights Review*, 1(2):124–139.

Institute of Medicine. 1993. *Veterans at Risk. The Health Effects of Mustard Gas and Lewisite.* Washington, D.C.: National Academy Press.

———. 2002. *Anthrax Vaccine. Is It Safe? Does It Work?* Washington, D.C.: National Academy Press.

Jackson, Paul J., Martin Hugh-Jones, D. M. Adair, G. Green et al. 1997. "PCR Analysis of Tissue Samples from the 1979 Sverdlovsk Anthrax Victims: The Presence of Multiple Bacillus anthracis Strains in Different Victims." *Proceedings of the National Academy of Sciences*, 179:818–824.

Malinowski, Bronislaw. 1948. *Magic, Science and Religion and Other Essays.* New York: Free Press.

Meselson, Matthew, Jeanne Guillemin, M. Hugh-Jones, Alexander Langmuir et al. 1994. "The Sverdlovsk Outbreak of 1979." *Science*, 266(5188):1202–1208.

Miller, Judith, Stephen Engelberg, and William Broad. 2001. *Germs, Biological Weapons and America's Secret War.* New York, NY: Simon and Schuster.

Pearson, Graham S. 1999. *The UNSCOM Saga: Chemical and Biological Weapons Non-Proliferation.* New York: St. Martin's Press.

Pomerantsev, A. P., N. A. Staritsin, L. I. Marinin, N. P. Kuzmin et al. 1995. "Immunomodulating Effect of Phospholipase C and Sphingomyelinase of Bacillus cereus in Protection against Anthrax." International workshop on Anthrax, Winchester, U.K., September 19–21.

Reuters News Service. 1998. "Anthrax Vaccine May Be Wishful Thinking," March 5.

Sidel, Victor S., Meryl Nass, and Todd Ensign. 1998. "The Anthrax Dilemma." *Medicine and Global Security*, 2(5):97–104.

Simmel, Georg. 1950. *The Sociology of Georg Simmel*. Kurt H. Walff, ed. New York, NY: Free Press.

Tuan, Yi-Fu. 1979. *Landscapes of Fear*. New York: Pantheon.

Turnbull, Peter C. B. 1991. "Anthrax Vaccines: Past, Present, and Future." *Vaccine*, 9:533–539.

U.S. Senate. 1994. "Staff Report for the Committee on Veterans' Affairs." Pp. 103–197. 103rd Congress. Washington, D.C.: Government Printing Office.

World Health Organization. 2003. "The Deliberate Release of Anthrax Spores Through the United States Postal System." In *Public Health Response to Biological and Chemical Weapons: Guidance from the World Health Organization*, Appendix 4.3. Pp. 76–81. Genova: WHO.

CHAPTER 3

Guardians of the Golden Age: Custodians of U.S. Military Culture

Pamela R. Frese

In this chapter I explore how anthropological concepts including residence patterns, descent systems, and fictive kin intersect with social class, race, and gender in American military culture. My analysis is based on the themes that emerged from the oral histories of fourteen white women now in their eighties whose husbands were high-ranking military officers during World War II and the Korean and Vietnam Wars. These women now make their home at The Heritage, a guarded "Life Care Community" designed for military officers and their wives. Two-thirds of the residents at The Heritage are married couples and a majority of the remaining residents are widows of military officers. These women are custodians of a Golden Age in American Military Culture, or, as one of my contributors explained, a time of the past and "the era of the big bands . . . the big wars, those two kind of go together. Back when we had Rosie the Riveter and all the people supported their country in this wartime era." The Golden Age is now a time of memory when "home" and "family" as gendered domains of power and influence were replicated in military stations around the world and are again reinvented here at The Heritage.

For these women, "home" has always been a series of different stations, a mobile residence that is reestablished wherever you have "family." And in stations where they did not have biological extended family, they relied on the nuclear family and a variety of fictive kin. One general's wife put it well: "Home is where the heart is, and the family. Moving around to many places in the world . . . homes change. Mobility is our way of life, and we learn that wherever we are, we make it 'home.'"

Realistically, there is not only one model of a military wife, but the women I interviewed are white, belong to the same socioeconomic class, and are united in age; they were children during World War I, and they all survived the Depression, World War II and the Korean, Vietnam, and Cold Wars. Several graduated from prestigious colleges before marriage and belonged to college sororities and other female social and charity organizations, such as the Daughters of the American Revolution (DAR), Army Daughters, the Red Cross, and the Junior League. Throughout their stories, the culturally prescribed roles for military officers and their wives and the importance of "homes" are intricately interwoven with elite Anglo American cultural ideals of patriotism, of dedication to country, and of the importance of the family.

This chapter explores these themes by providing, first, a brief history of the women who marry into the U.S. military and become military wives and mothers. Next, through selections from the oral histories I collected with fourteen retired military wives, I help them to describe their own experiences of the "military family" in their youth and in marriage to a U.S. military officer. Finally, I share a more recent picture of their lives in the "military family" at The Heritage.

The Heritage and Anthropological Methods

The Heritage is managed by an international hotel corporation.[1] This retirement community is located on the East Coast of the United States with easy access to the social and cultural life offered by a nearby major metropolitan center besides the opportunities available to residents of suburban life with malls, convenience stores, and Wal-Mart. Residents of The Heritage also rely on the facilities provided by several military bases in the surrounding area. The residential community includes cottages and apartments for independent living, one- or two-person suites set aside for assisted living, and a Health Care Center. The residents in the Health Care Center are those who need around-the-clock medical assistance due to a recent hospital visit; those permanent residents who suffer from forms of dementia; and, finally, those who are dying. My mother died in a room there on a cold gray morning in February 1997.

The Heritage is a special community, modeled on a tradition proudly linked to the military and to the government of the United States. Special ties are celebrated to the early days of the United States during the Revolution for Independence and expansion into the western frontiers. The residence buildings are named after four U.S. Presidents who were among the founders of America: Adams, Jefferson, Madison, and Washington. Pictures in the public area include framed prints of illustrious military men who were heroes of the Revolutionary and Civil wars, foxes and hounds in the countryside, and beautiful scenes of nature and colonial mansions nestled in carefully sculpted gardens. The public rooms at The Heritage are expensively furnished and reflect spaces similar to those found in a five-star hotel. In this residential community, the presence of guards at the gate, the use of space within the community, the continued ties to old friends and family in everyday life, and the fictive kin relationships established with the staff work together to provide a familiar and comfortable lifestyle for the residents.

Residents of The Heritage described their "home" as their most recent "post" in a long line of assignments; as a secured "compound" that provides safety from the outside, somewhat foreign, world; or as an executive suite in a "five-star resort hotel" with fine dining similar to that in other fine hotels in other parts of the world. The most frequent description of The Heritage that all my contributors shared was its resemblance to a traditional military "home" where family and friends could socialize, much like the supportive ties found in life on a military post of the past.

The Heritage is modeled loosely after military posts located in the United States and abroad; guarded temporary homes that were generally separated from the local indigenous communities. During the historic time in which these women served as active military wives, a military post was "by necessity a self-sufficient community, it might be compared to a small town," and on these posts "Shopping and marketing are often made convenient.... There are also concessions for a beauty shop, barber shop, and a shoe repair service.... A library and a hobby shop can generally be found in some niche of every post" (Shea 1966 [1941]:72, 74). The re-creation of the "post" or "small town" dimension of the Golden Age is intentional. Indeed, residents at The Heritage have selected a multivocal residential space that re-images a special time of the past. They can "buy" a moment from the life during which they were in control of the world. But there are multiple ways to interpret The Heritage and its manipulation of social time.

The Resident Services Manager of the Heritage told me that "The Heritage is a Continuing Care Retirement Community where the people who qualify to live here, the military retirees as I call them, can live comfortably with the camaraderie that they were used to when they were in active duty. They still have that same atmosphere that they enjoyed for so many years. This makes it very pleasant for them to live in this environment; it's their home. When people retire they like that small hometown atmosphere. They like to know Joe on the corner, or the barber down the street, or this gal who's in the country store now."

One advertising brochure for The Heritage describes the significant feature of this retirement community as a practically self-sufficient "small town": "The major features of the Community Center include a lobby with concierge desk, fine dining facilities with accommodations for private dining, living room, library, auditorium, gift shop, coffee shop/convenience store, barber shop, beauty parlor, bank, exercise room, therapeutic whirlpool, heated indoor swimming pool, arts and crafts room, woodworking shop, chapel and a computer activity center. Outdoor recreational facilities include tennis courts, walking trails, putting green, golf driving cage, gazebo, fishing dock, horseshoe pit and picnic area" (Heritage brochure n.d., ca.1995).

Residents at The Heritage have chosen this option for final retirement over others. As another administrator explained: "Many of the [residents] did a variety of other things when they left the military and before they fully retired. Somebody's at World Bank, somebody's at AT&T, a lot of big business type of things. But here they're known as captain, major, general, colonel and that's the common bond that brings them together."

The weekly newsletter produced for the residents outlines many of the social and cultural events sponsored by The Heritage. These include classes and self-help workshops on various aspects of the residents' health: walking and water exercise groups, aerobics classes, support groups for particular illnesses and physical disabilities, and a regular discussion group on general "Health Concerns." Regular organized games for community residents include poker, bridge, mahjong, Scrabble, and bingo. Residents can choose to participate in organized groups of artists, writers, and in a theatre guild. These groups share their work with the larger community through displays in the art gallery and in public performances. There are several weekly showings of popular movies, happy hours, sing-alongs, and dance parties. The Heritage designs special events to celebrate national holidays or community celebrations organized around particular themes, such as a Hawaiian luau, a German night, a Japanese celebration, and a festival to honor Scottish and New England traditions. These celebrations are especially welcomed, as many residents served in the military in those countries or can trace their descent to ancestors from there. The Heritage regularly offers shopping trips to a variety of stores and shuttles to surrounding medical facilities. The residents also can take advantage of planned excursions that include trips to local restaurants, to centers for the fine arts, and deluxe overnight trips to historic sites. The Heritage provides private facilities for parties and receptions, including receptions after the funerals of deceased community members.

I observed that the staff of The Heritage is personable and polite to the residents. The general manager had direct ties to the U.S. military and had been decorated for his military service in Vietnam. All of the administrators with whom I had dealings are white. The waiters and waitresses are generally African and African American. The maids I met, who clean each residence once a week, are generally from El Salvador and Mexico. From what I could see, the maintenance and grounds crews are drawn from these groups as well. I have been told that in the last few years many Vietnamese have taken these positions. In any event, the resident manager commented, "The residents say to me, 'All of the people who work here, you are like a family to us and we're very secure in the mind that you're here.' "

I first learned of The Heritage after my grandmother's death in December 1990. My mother's mother, my Grandma Lester, had come to live with us after my grandfather's death in the early 1970s. After Grandma's death and because my mother's health was declining, my parents decided that they really didn't need the five-bedroom family home anymore. My father is a retired Air Force lieutenant colonel and my parents were able to afford the down payment, so they elected to move into an independent living cottage at The Heritage in 1990. Their cottage was a 1,358-square-foot "Plan R" with a living room, a formal dining room with chandelier, an eat-in kitchen, two bedrooms, two baths, and a den. It was beautiful and full of light.

When I decided to begin my research with women who lived at The Heritage, I relied on oral histories as windows into the rich experiences of women whose lives remain relatively hidden from public view. Many recent anthropological texts address the multifaceted nature of nonwhite, subaltern women's life stories (Abu-Lughod 1993; Baker 1998; Behar 1993; Patai 1988; Prieto 1997; Randall 1995 [1981], 1994). The women I met appear, in one way, to belong to a privileged race and class within the United States. But their world, too, is hidden from most members of American society, even though these women have played a significant role in American society. Through their life histories, we see how different generation of women adapt to, and sometimes intentionally subvert, their prescribed gender roles.

And as a scholar seeking to understand a special worldview through the memories of those who lived it, I also relied on participant observation. Often I met one or more of these women at special events at The Heritage: at a poetry reading or a magician's performance in the ballroom; at a Christmas party in a private home; or perhaps during a privately catered celebration in the art gallery of the main community building. I visited with them in various places: the library, the pool, the exercise room, and during meals in the dining room. I began to attend receptions and parties in other residents' homes. My children caught tadpoles in the stocked fish pond. We walked the paved track that encircles the pond and watched the Canadian Geese, Purple Martins, and Blue Birds that are constant visitors there. We went to church on Sundays in the auditorium. We spent our afternoons at the pool. I will always remember my mother sitting by the side of the pool in her wheelchair, smiling encouragement to her grandchildren and sometimes dozing off in the moist heat. We participated in much the same way as all the other residents' children and grandchildren did, except that my father had been in the Air Force, while most of the residents had served in the Army.

I met several of the women through my parents, especially my mother. In addition, I offered two community presentations on my research with Anglo American culture. At each presentation, I solicited volunteers who were interested in having their life histories recorded. I met many of my contributors through these presentations.

Interviews took place in each lady's living room. When I visited in most of their homes, I felt as if I were sitting in the parlor of a fine old mansion or, perhaps, in a display of a fine home carefully constructed by a museum curator to house important artifacts of American and world culture. There were always framed photographs of family members on the walls and table tops; frequently these displays included photographs of each woman's husband in the company of at least one, and sometimes three, American presidents and other world leaders. Each woman knows some of the family stories attached to all her fine artifacts—the antique imported and American furniture, the figurines, china, crystal, and oil paintings displayed throughout the rooms. These objects crystallize memories of a life's experiences and form the most obvious threads to unite generations since they are destined to be passed on as heirlooms to family members or to museums and/or endowments to charities. Our conversations frequently were stimulated by the memories attached to these objects, as time markers that prompted stories of the past.

The women I worked with still contribute to the reproduction of contemporary U.S. society in important ways. They sit on national boards of religious and philanthropic organizations. They continue to participate in the DAR and in Army Daughters. They volunteer in local churches and schools, and they regularly visit residents of the healthcare center. These women continue to influence their children's, grandchildren's, and great-grandchildren's understanding of the world through family celebrations, through the passing of heirlooms, and through their stories about life. In fact, they are an important part of an aristocratic culture that heavily relies on women to reproduce particular constructions of gender, family, and the Anglo American way of life in a variety of ways.

The Officer's Wife in American Culture

Alt and Stone (1991) explain how the early American military was filled with officers drawn primarily from the wealthy landowner or merchant class and was distinct from the enlisted or "serving class" of soldiers. At Valley Forge in 1777, officers' wives "dodged bullets, nursed the wounded, foraged for food, cooked, knitted garments for the men, and served as water and ammunition carriers. Beginning the service wives' tradition of placing the needs of the military first, they maintained some semblance of domestic life and became an essential thread in the historical tapestry of the American military system" (Alt and Stone 1991:1 and 2). The authors credit Mrs. Washington with forming the first Officers' Wives' Club at Valley Forge, where "the tradition was being set for officers' wives to entertain for their husbands" (Alt and Stone 1991: 11). These early social gatherings provided women with a support system or "sisterhood" of wives at every military post where they might be stationed.

And after the Revolutionary War, cultural practices and beliefs in high-ranking military culture and in the elite of Anglo American society still overlapped. Officers' wives were frequently drawn from upper-class families and, with their husbands, formed teams to reestablish an American "aristocracy" in which "most officers were graduates of West Point or Annapolis. Many carried on a family tradition of several generations of men in arms, and many had personal incomes aside from their military pay" (Alt and Stone 1991:85). Military wives participated in the perpetuation of a military social class or "caste-like" system; for wives: "No matter what her background or schooling, if a woman married an officer, she became a part of the aristocracy which the army created and reinforced" (Alt and Stone 1991:48).

Many women who became officers' wives before World War II were raised within elite white civilian society, while others were proud members of a military family and were continuing in their ancestors' commitment to the nation. Women's roles in both elite civilian and high-ranking military society included active participation as unpaid labor in the public sphere within a variety of religious and philanthropic institutions. And regardless of their own patrilineal ties to elite or military society, a military officer's wife has always been required to be successful in the reproduction of home, children, and the larger military family wherever her husband was stationed.

Shea's manual for Army wives (1941) articulated several important dimensions to the role of a military wife that included loyalty to her family, to the Army, and to the honor of the United States:

> So you are with the Army now!! As a wife you have a most important role in your husband's Army career. . . . His work will reflect his life at home,

your attitude toward the Army, your interest in his duty, and your adapt-ability. In this respect, you also have an important part in our national security, and a duty to your country....Although no serviceman's career was ever *made* by his wife, many have been hindered or helped by the social skills of their wives, their flexibility, and their loyalty toward the Army and its customs. It is your responsibility to create the right back-ground for your husband and your ability to do so can make a subtle but important contribution to his advancement. (Shea 1966 [1941]:52; emphasis in original)

A military wife had a rank in relation to other military wives that paralleled that of her husband, and an officer's career was successful, in part, because of his wife's abilities and performance within the female hierarchy. Wives were expected to join the volunteer army of women that rooted the military base in a particular place and time. They certainly were expected to participate in the Officers' Wives' Clubs, the Red Cross, and other organizations designed to benefit members of their extended military "family," including the thrift shop and the nursery. As members of the Officers' Wives' Club, women played bridge, hosted teas and receptions, and helped to provide educational and cultural programs for the larger community of women, including lower-ranking U.S. military wives and the wives of the local political and social elite. Women were discouraged from taking paid employment that might conflict with their other obligations as members of the larger military family. Besides this volunteer work, the contributors to my study explained that a successful wife especially needed to cultivate the domestic sphere where her home, children, and even her domestic help required her special skills.

The Military "Family"

The concept of "family" in the military culture that is most familiar to these women is inclusive, incorporating a woman's nuclear and extended families and a variety of very important fictive kin relationships. And these kinds of "family" flow through different times for each woman, beginning with their own childhood all the way to their residence at The Heritage. Women may have been raised in military families or simply married into them, but their descriptions of family ties speak their active reproduction of the American spirit and the frontier ethic.

Connections to the Military and Elite Culture before Marriage

Most of the women with whom I worked had been born into a military fam-ily. Mrs. Cantrell explained: "I was born into the Army in Vancouver,

Washington, in 1916. My father was a military dentist. He went overseas during the war, staffing an American hospital. Mother had the frontier attitude. I mean, Daddy's off fighting a war, and let's keep the home fires burning. But it certainly wasn't a new thing even then. When Dad did get back, she made a home wherever he was moved." Mrs. Gentry smiled as she remembered:

> I thoroughly enjoyed the time in the Philippines. My father was in command of the hospital at Fort Stotsenburg. My mother's brother had graduated from West Point and had come to Fort Stotsenburg while we were there. He was Post Adjutant. He lived at one end of the parade ground with his family and we lived at the other. So I had my three first cousins living at the other end of the parade ground. . . . I would play golf with my mother and my father. And we'd go horseback riding. . . . When my father was stationed in Washington D.C.. . . . I went to senior high school at Western High School. It was loaded with Army, Navy, and diplomatic children. A few well-to-do civilian children who weren't going to private school also went to Western . . . I lived in the area called Foxhall Village in northwest Washington. Foxhall Village was *loaded* with military people. On both sides of us lived military people. There was somebody who lived behind us that my mother had known before. And up the street were girls and boys who went to Western when I did, who were military kids. . . . Some of the people who went to Western with me live here at The Heritage right now.

Mrs. Spokesman proudly remembered:

> Having been born into the Army in 1918, during World War I when my father was stationed at Camp Grant, Illinois. I grew up as a typical "Army Brat." After the war, my parents chose to remain in the service, rather than returning to my father's law firm in Chicago. . . . Life in the Philippines was, for me, more like living at a country club: swimming, tennis, golf, horses to ride, and frequent dances.

Mrs. Wilson explained: "I was born at West Point. My father graduated from West Point in the Class of 1908 and was back at West Point serving as an assistant professor in the math department. Then Dad was stationed in the Presidio of San Francisco." Mrs. Gentry said:

> My mother's father became an Army doctor. So they were all over the place all their lives. My father was born in a small town near Columbus,

Ohio. After he had gone to medical school, he became a reserve officer and was sent to Washington, D.C. to go to Army medical school. He became a regular Army officer in 1910. My mother was always beaming, and you could tell that all her life as an Army child she had enjoyed herself and had had a wonderful time. All of us always had a great time.

Mrs. White explained that

I was born in San Francisco, and we went immediately by boat to Hawaii. My father was stationed in Pearl Harbor. My father's father was a rancher in the Far West. He had two very large ranches and had cattle runs from the ranch, which was in Texas, up to the ranch in Wyoming. And my father, before he decided he wanted to become a doctor, used to ride with those [cattle runs]. I think those were some of the happiest times that he had—he loved it. . . . My mother had absolutely no use for my father's family, because she was brought up in Paris and went to finishing schools in Florence and Berlin.

Mrs. Cantrell told me that:

You always had a roof over your head in the Army, and you always had plenty of food, but there were things you couldn't afford to do unless you had outside income. My father's sister and her husband were in the military. They were the ones who lived next door to me at West Point. Their two sons were in the military, my mother and father were in the military—and this one civilian engineer and his wife, you see, were the anchor. So, if the wife couldn't follow the husband someplace, they'd go to my aunt. . . . My mother's sister was the only one with any money in the whole family, everybody else was in the Army life. She lived up on the side of a hill in Maplewood, New Jersey, and it looked out over the town of Maplewood. I went and lived with my aunt and uncle and attended, as a day student, a very good girls' school, Kent Place, out in New Jersey.

Whether or not the women I interviewed were born into a military family or were raised as children of elite white society, these women proudly described their parents, their early family life, and their ancestors' connections to the founding of the United States. Mrs. Spokesman related: "My family goes back to the Revolution. As a matter of fact, my ancestors were here over a hundred years before the Revolution. The first ones landed in Jamestown, Virginia, on the ship America. They became staunch

Virginians." And Mrs. Smith explained that "I was born in Baltimore on the twenty second of December in 1929. My family on my mother's side came from the land grant families of Maryland. Part of her family is from the Eastern Shore and the other part is from Southern Maryland. They go back to the early history of founding the colony in Maryland." Mrs. McCloud retells the Horatio Algier story intertwined with her own father's history:

> Everybody in my family, way back, has always been wealthy enough to live well. They were all fine people.... My father had lost most of his money during the crash, and he was just absolutely falling apart. Mother said to him, "Well, you made money before, you can do it again." And he did—he died as a millionaire. He had been a farm boy without any money. His father gave him a dollar and told him to leave home and make his way. That's all he could give him. He went to architecture school by mail and worked during the day—and was a really a self-made man, very much admired by all his friends.

Regardless of whether the women were born into a military family, or were raised in elite Anglo American culture, they all married an officer in the U.S. military.

Marriage into the Military

Several of the ladies met their future husbands through a variety of kin networks. Mrs. Wilson explained that "I was through college, and Mrs. Emery wrote Mother and invited me to come over and stay with them. The second night after I got there, Mrs. Emery had several young lieutenants to a dinner party. My date was my future husband. We became engaged finally, two or three weeks after I met him. We were married in '38, and we're coming up on fifty-seven years." And Mrs. Cooper said,

> I had a cousin who lived at West Point with her husband. Her mother and my mother were first cousins and they were like sisters, they grew up together. My cousin's mother kept writing her to invite me to West Point, and my mother kept writing me to see if I was interested in going. I went and I think my cousin bribed those lieutenants into coming to dinner and meeting me. My husband-to-be was one of them. He came down to New York a few weeks later, and we went out to dinner and then he invited me back to West Point, and one thing led to another. He was an English instructor. He had been at West Point for three years.

Researchers have shown that civilian high-society and high-ranking military leaders have shared membership in an "aristocratic" culture since the Revolutionary War, especially through intermarriage (see Alt and Stone [1991]). Most of the wives I interviewed were married to men who continue to celebrate their membership in age grades of graduating classes from prestigious military academies. West Point and Annapolis, for example, are located near respected eastern schools for women and prescribed cross-dating ensured that women of the educated upper classes met and married the men who were destined to be high-ranking future officers of the U.S. military. When a woman became engaged and then married an officer, she became a member in a sisterhood of women who had married her husband's age mates. Mrs. Smith said that "the Naval Academy Miniature goes with the wedding band. Just as the men cherish their rings from West Point and Annapolis and the Air Force Academy, we ladies do, too. They're kind of a badge in the sorority."

A wife's position within multiple kin networks was reproduced anew at every posting. Mrs. Cantrell said:

> We had a funny little house at Schofield that had been noncommissioned quarters in World War I. It was one bedroom. My first child was born there in 1938. We put the baby in the one bedroom, and I tacked up the waterproof covering around the screens and moved on the porch; that was our bedroom. My cousin lived next door. He was a classmate of my husband. It was a very friendly area, very friendly. That was a good way to get started in married life. You know when you have good company a lot of things aren't very important.

A wife continued to rely on her own kin who were members of influential American culture. When her husband was overseas, Mrs. Smith

> went up to Baltimore and stayed with my family for a while. My mother didn't drive a car, so she was happy to have me taking her to tea parties for the Ladies Eastern Shore Society or the DAR. My father had a retail business that he had inherited from his father and that my brother is now operating. It's over a hundred years old; a horse and stable supplies, a saddlery. My brother was riding at that time with the United States Equestrian Team, so I came up for horse shows and went up to Canada with the family and the shows up there, and that kind of thing.

Membership in Women's Groups: Officers' Wives' Clubs

All the women who participated in my research were active in Officers' Wives' Clubs at every new posting. This Club provided all officers' wives with opportunities to socialize with women in similar social positions at the post. These women were the members of an elite group who were unofficially given the duties parallel to their husbands' rank in the informal running of the base. The Wives' Clubs provided a support network for officers' wives and their families and created the bridge to the elite women in the local, civilian society.

An officer's wife was also given responsiblity for the women married to the men under her husband's command. This supervision of women "under her" included the proper education in military etiquette and in appropriate gender roles traditionally associated with the Anglo American upper class. Fictive ties with lower ranking women positioned the ranking wife as "mother" to the wives of the men in her husband's command. Mrs. Smith captures many dimensions of this role:

> I was active with the Officers' Wives Club. There was always a purpose and a guest speaker; a charity of some sort, some reason for the organization. The Wives' Club ran the thrift shop, and they ran several on-post activities of that sort. I worked at the hospital for the Red Cross as a Gray Lady. We used to plan entertaining programs, bingo games and movies, and that sort of thing, push bookmobiles around, and feed the babies— just general help. And, of course, we felt an obligation to the enlisted families. My husband had several married men that he took with him over there [overseas] and I felt it important that I keep in touch with those ladies; some of them had children. So those women whose husbands had gone kind of formed a little enclave, and we'd go to dinner together… that was one of the biggest inducements in the military life, the camaraderie. You never needed anything at all; you always had somebody around you, even if you were miles and miles away from your own family, you always had family.

Mrs. McCloud explained that "my husband had the regiment at Jackson, so I had all the ladies in the regiment to watch over. I tried to go see the new babies, and take care that somebody who was sick had everything they needed; kind of tried to be a mother, you know, to them all. There was plenty to do. And then I'd put on programs once a month at the Officers' Club." Mrs. Wilson remembered that "you tried to teach the military wives the etiquette of the nation in which they were stationed—you had to learn it yourself. We also trained the wives how to be ladies, or help them a little bit; a few of them needed it."

The obligations for the commanding generals' wives entailed entertaining local and foreign diplomats and military leaders and building bonds with their wives. Mrs. Wilson continued:

> My husband was a general and was the chief of staff to the commanding general, and I got to be sort of the general's wife's aide. She just said, "Now, I want you to make sure the Women's Club gets organized . . . our purpose here is to try and show how we do things in America. And I want the Turkish ladies incorporated—brought—into this Women's Club so they can see that the women in America do something besides sit on a cushion and do a fine seam." It was not an unpleasant job . . . we were always included in things that the general was. Socially, we did not meet anybody but the highly educated and very wealthy. They were charming, many of them; the wives of the influential military heads.

Mrs. Cooper explained that in Japan, "my husband was commanding general and so I became honorary president of the women's group and had coffees and teas and things of that kind to get the wives together. Our Women's Club sponsored Japanese plays and fashion shows. I had obligations but I always made time for the hospital work."

Mrs. Cantrell remembered that when "my husband was assigned overseas to Cairo, Egypt, my French came in very handy. There were lots of people in the Women's Club, and I was advised to get to know the other nationalities who were stationed there. English or French was the common denominator. I could talk to the Hungarian attaché's wife, and it made conversation easier. That helped me make special friendships with many women that I still have today."

Fictive Kin Relationships with Domestic Help

The women with whom I spoke envisioned a world in which their relations with domestic help frequently took on kin-like attributes. Within the United States, domestic help was usually enlisted men and their wives. Mrs. Gentry explained:

> At Fort Belvoir [Virginia], a young enlisted man's wife worked for us. When he and [my husband] were both ordered to Richmond Air Base, he

and his wife lived in a big basement room in our house, and she again was our servant. The enlisted man's wife did the cooking and the cleaning and I did the baby tending.... In Germany the servant assigned to us was Hildegard, and I really liked her very much. She had a little girl who was about the age of my children and Hildegard used to bring her daughter to work with her. I would take her little girl and my two little boys swimming. Hildegard would stay home and clean house and cook and do things like that.

Mrs. Bartlett also created fictive kin ties to aid her in managing the domestic sphere: "Quarters were difficult for women alone. One of the sergeant's wives wanted a place to live, and we took her in. If I had to be away, she was there to cover. She helped me with the cooking, and we were mutually helpful to each other. Her marriage did not last after the war, but she remarried—we've kept in touch through all the years." And Mrs. Smith recounts that when her daughter was born,

> I got household help. The gal that started working for me had a husband who was Air Force, and when he came back from Japan she went off with him. But her aunt came to work for me, and stayed with me all the way through from the time Roxanne was six months old until we moved here; and even at that she came back to my daughter's wedding. I could leave the kids with her and go do my shopping. They were of the _____ family, a long time founding Negro family of Severna Park [Maryland]. They owned a large portion of land. In their many generations they kept passing the land on. She's been very close to us through the years.

Many women grew up with inherited family ties to families of nonwhite or lower-class domestic workers. Mrs. Cooper explained:

> At the apartment we had Martha Jackson to come in and clean when I was young. Martha was black and just a young girl when she started. She was about two years older than I, and almost a member of the family. I remember her very well because she continued to work for my mother and grandmother until my grandmother died. Then my mother [and Martha] came to me during the war, [while] I was living in Macon with my children when my husband was overseas. Our Martha was a wonderful person. I helped her financially until she died just a couple years ago. I was not alone in the financial support, my cousins also helped. I always went to see her when I visited Macon. She retired and had a nice house with a garden. Yes, I loved Martha dearly.

Mrs. White avowed that

> I would not be married unless Rubel could come. Rubel was a character who had a great deal of influence with us. He was a black man, and a very elderly one at that point. His mother was my great-grandmother's slave. My great-grandmother and great-grandfather were very pro-North; they were not southerners, although Kansas City, Missouri, was southern. They were very much antislavery but they did have a couple of slaves, as was common in those days. They freed them all and put them on a salary. They freed Rubel's mother but she wouldn't go; she stayed with them until she died. And she had Rubel who was a member of the family as far as we were concerned. I used to count on Rubel for everything, including advice. He had a family, and he sent them all to college. We helped fund some of it, and we paid Rubel a salary. I'll always remember Rubel. Rubel showed up immaculate in a black tie and tuxedo and he served us champagne. It must have been quite an effort for him to come to do that, you know, because he was very old, and I don't think he was all that well at that point.

Mrs. Classer described how she went with their two children to join her husband and:

> My husband met me at the train when we arrived with two servants, Naomi and JC. The maid, Naomi, whom I had not known before, turned out to be a jewel. She was very precious to us. Naomi called Julia, the baby, her "baby doll." She loved our daughter. Naomi did the cooking. She was an American Negro. She had a room in our house and lived with us most of the time, and then would go home to her family on the weekends.... And JC. He was my husband's caddie at the golf club. He brought JC home one day after JC had caddied for him because we were having a barbecue party out in our yard, and he wanted JC to help him. Well, JC ended staying the rest of the time we were in Fort McClellan. He lived in our basement. We paid him very slim wages but he got all his meals with us.... He was an American Negro. He was an orphan, the youngest of a large family. He had been passed around from one brother or sister to another. JC did chores around the house and jobs like cutting the grass, and bringing in the wood for the fireplace, and emptying ashes, and things of that sort. Eventually he moved to Detroit, but we kept in touch with him. Later when my husband began to write books, he was sent around to different towns to talk about his books at book sales and things. He was sent to Detroit, and JC's daughter found out somehow that he was going to be the speaker there, and she came to see my

husband and took him to see JC. So we kept in touch with him for many years.

One other excellent example of this kind of fictive kin relationship was shared by Mrs. Bartlett:

I did have good help with me in my home life. Mary came to us from the Woman's Exchange, the leader of which was one of our church members. It was a hiring agency of the very finest kind. Mary was a wonderful black woman, who was just nineteen when we came to Washington. She came to live with us as I had the little month-old baby when we arrived, so I very much needed her. She has been a blessing to us all the way through, and I think we mean a lot to her, too. She had come to Washington and left her little baby at home with her wonderful mother. So Mary came into our lives, and she lived in the servant's room on the third floor, which was all set up for that, with its own little bath. Missing her little child so much she just took over our little baby, Clara, and, really, she was her mother through all those years. They have a close, close loving relationship. . . . She is like my family, and she is an important member. She even came back to help me when we moved here to The Heritage.

Outside of the United States, domestic help was most frequently "passed down" from other officers' wives who had been reassigned to another post and were leaving their staff behind. Or servants may have "come with the house" that the military officer's family was assigned overseas.

Mrs. Wilson explained that in Germany after the war,

Most of the servants you got would have been working for another American. The other American would get ordered home and know you're looking for a maid—somebody who can wait tables, make beds, talk English, and take care of the children. As a family would leave, they would make known the fact that their help was going to need a new job. And that's how—you just kind of passed them. We had a nursemaid because our youngest child, Bob, was eighteen months old and we had social business to do. Her name was Irna. She was a delightful person, and for many years I corresponded with her. She was like family.

In Hawaii, Mrs. McCloud "found the most wonderful little Japanese maid. She had been working for the general's wife, who was returning to the States. She wore her kimonos and flitted around the house like a butterfly, singing. And, oh, she was just precious. Her name was Joi. And she adored the babies, and she was just like a second mother to them. . . . Joi lived in quarters right behind me—they had servants' quarters."

Mrs. Cantrell described how

> We lived in a bungalow in the Philippines. One wing was the servants' quarters. There was a *lavandera*, a washwoman, who pounded your clothes against the stone floor; the cook, José, who came from the southern island; and Doroteo the houseboy, who scooted around with rags tied to his feet to clean the nice wood floors. They just came with the house. Whoever lived with the house had them, which was kind of nice. The servants never had to move, they knew the peculiarities of the house. . . . When we moved to Egypt, our house was reserved by the American Embassy for their attachés. In other words it was staffed already, we didn't have to rustle up a good cook or a good houseman, and it was much simpler that way.

Mrs. Parker, a general's wife, spoke of her household in Thailand where she found her staff through friends. In addition, "[My husband] sent for Sergeant Jefferson, who had been with him in Washington and Vietnam, to watch over us. He came and he brought his family; his wife and three sons. They were black, and we loved them dearly and they were with us for ten years. It was just like my family."

"Family" in Retirement

After their husbands retired from the military, most of the wives I interviewed continued to rely on a variety of kinship networks. Mrs. McCloud said that in retirement, she and her husband returned to live near her own natal family roots:

> When my husband retired and we came back to Maryland to live, I belonged to five different flower groups. I joined a garden club that my mother and sister had been president of, and which I became president of. I belonged to the Horticulture Society of Maryland and Ikebana International, the Japanese art of flower arrangement. Then my sister started a group called the Guild of Flower Artisans—that was attached to the Baltimore Museum of Art, and we'd often be asked to do arrangements that complemented various art portraits and paintings. I joined the DAR and I was on five boards of various groups, including the Children's Hospital.

Mrs. Spokesman explained how she continued in active roles in many women's organizations:

> I was active in the Daughters of the United States Army. I had served as president of the Fort Benning chapter (1954–1956), then later as national president for two terms (1976–1980). I also served as chaplain of the local chapter of the DAR for five years and as the scholarship chairman for two years. I have also maintained my lifelong membership in the Pi Beta Phi Alumnae Association and, later, the Colonial Dames XVII Century.

And Mrs. Gentry, like many other wives at The Heritage, belongs "to the Daughters of U.S. Army. I belong to the state chapter. I'm on the national board. We meet at each other's houses and usually take a sandwich and the hostess gives us some tea and a piece of cake or a cookie for dessert."

The glimpses of the military "family" just provided belong to the women who now live at The Heritage. But why do they live here? How is this special place able to capture and manipulate time and "family" for its residents?

The Move to the "Family" at The Heritage

Residents choose to live at The Heritage for a variety of reasons, many of which relate directly to the mobile "military family" and American pioneer roots. Mrs. Spokesman said, "We watched the Heritage Retirement Home being built. In 1989 we became pioneers and were the first residents to move into the Jefferson Building. And here we still are, nine years later, living in this beautiful retirement home with other elderly residents, many of whom are old friends from our long years in the Army who speak our language. Sometimes it feels that we've never left the Army."

Mrs. Bartlett also "discovered that we had many friends here. The general manager, we had known as a little boy. We knew his uncle and auntie, who had lived at the Westchester and served Eisenhower as Secretary of the Army at the time. They came to our church and were very active church people."

Mrs. Cantrell reflected that

> My age group was very lucky to have support systems wherever you go. We kept in touch, 'cause we were all moving. . . . Some of those boys from my youth at West Point are right here in this building; old buddies of mine from those days. When my friends kept urging me to come out here, the thing that won their point was that these are the old friends I can talk to about my family . . . and I got Christmas cards from all my

husband's 1935 classmates' wives who said "We're all going to move there, come and join us." So I thought, "why not?" I have, even to this day, fifteen wives of classmates of my husband's here, all of whom I have known a lifetime. And I thought, "That's the support system I really need." You share so many memories, and you can always say, "Hey, I need help," and they're more than happy to oblige.

Mrs. Gentry was attracted to the unity of the military "family" at The Heritage when, after her husband's death,

I came here by myself. There are a lot of 1935 widows here at The Heritage, of which I am one, and when I first came it seemed like a good idea to call each other up early in the morning to check on each other. Three of us called each other up. Then a fourth one came and four of us call each other up, but now there are a lot more than that. I think other people do the same thing now too—little check up groups. Everyday we call each other up at eight o'clock in the morning...it's like having sisters.

Mrs. Cooper explained that

My husband and I had signed up for The Heritage together when it was just a dream. He died before the construction started. I came to The Heritage very early, so I moved in here with the pioneers. My daughter helped me move. There were only about fifty residents when I moved in. The Madison and Jefferson were the only buildings that were finished and the Jefferson really wasn't completely ready. They were still painting and buckets, ladders, and things were in the halls. There was no water in the lake, no roads. We were really pioneers. I've made some wonderful friends. I have a few friends that I had known before. But most of them are people I've met since I've been here. So many from earlier years have passed away. I miss them.

Mrs. Wilson explained that "This is, theoretically, the last stop. The Heritage. My husband was on the committee to build the place, and we moved into the Adams when it was brand new. My husband is more comfortable if he has men in his general age bracket who have done the things that he has done...and I like the women. It's a comfortable family feeling."

Some widows at The Heritage have no living biological family, and many take an active role in creating "family" with the help of the staff at

The Heritage. Mrs. White provides an excellent example, when she recalled:

> My husband died in 1989, and I moved into The Heritage. When I first came here, I was very lonely, because I had just lost my husband, and I was trying to move into a community where I knew only three people. Christmas and holidays are always dreadful things for people who are lonely, and a new widow. I scoured around and I saw a lot of people who had no family, people who I liked. I thought, "Why don't I ask them over for Christmas dinner?" Now, I hate cooking, so I called up The Heritage and I said, "I need a turkey for so many people, and I need the dressing and all the junk that goes with it." Then everybody got in the spirit of things. Every Christmas I have up to twenty-seven people to a sit-down Christmas dinner here at the cottage; it is a crowded, intimate gathering.

I began this chapter with a promise of what traditional anthropological concepts can offer to today's world, especially in trying to understand the multifaceted relationship among the constructions of gender, race, class, and the U.S. military culture. Certainly the continuous recreation of "family" and "home" in a necessarily mobile society requires an important reliance on the role of blood ties, marriage relationships, and fictive kin to help the military family to reproduce "home" anywhere in the world. Diversity in terms of race, ethnicity, and class were subsumed under the creation of fictive kin relationships during their careers as active duty officers' wives. Anthropologists never downplay fictive kin ties; the strength of age set membership to compete with lineage ties is well documented. Men and women at The Heritage celebrate fictive kinship-like relationships, many of which have existed for over eighty years. And both men and women who now live at The Heritage create fictive kin relationships anew with other residents and the staff in the retirement community. They have chosen to live with lifelong friends and to replicate fictive kin ties with staff at The Heritage that resemble their relationships with hired help throughout their lives.

These wives are active guardians for this complicated form of "kin work" that underlies the reproduction of a gendered hegemonic structure wherever the U.S. military can be found, even in retirement and old age. Strict adherents to this perspective might position white male officers at the top of a hierarchy under which their wives, enlisted men and their wives, and indigenous non-white civilian personnel could be ranked. High-ranking wives become "sisters" to other officers' wives and to women who are members of the political and military elite of the country in which her husband is stationed. "Kin work," as Di Leonardi (1992) discovered, relies on women to maintain kinship networks and intergenerational ties within a particular ethnicity in the United States. Military "kin work" especially revolves around the multiple meanings associated with an officer's wife's role as "mother." Above all, officers' wives produce children and provide them with an education and moral outlook. At the same time, some "mother work" associated with the rearing of children is passed to lower-ranking and/or indigenous women. The women at The Heritage continue to function as organizers and major participants in social and "kin" events in their residential community. They are the "Welcome Wagon" to new residents and especially contact the wife with gifts and invitations to join in the community. Women are usually the ones to visit the sick and volunteer in the Health Care Center. In addition, these women participate as active members in local church congregations; remain active in the DAR, Army Daughters, and other philanthropic groups; and organize excursions to historical and foreign places. These social roles are very similar to those in which they participated before retirement (see Collins 1992; Daniels 1988).

Their stories describe the powerful construction of "family" and "residence" that are an important part of how retired military wives remember the past. Their stories are memories: clusters of remembered lives that help them relive the past while living in a special kind of museum, guarded from the outside world. These women shared important parts of their lives with me through their narratives, multivocal slices of memory that perhaps reflect an idealized image of the past. Stephanie Coontz (1992) beautifully illustrates how memories of traditional family life become like myths, harmonizing discord and painting many complex relationships with a fine and sympathetic artist's brush. One thing, however, is certainly true. Their stories, whether historically correct accounts of the past or not, actively contribute to the celebration and the reproduction of an American aristocracy that is dedicated to the service of ancestors, country, and God.

Notes

I am very grateful to The College of Wooster for support of my research through Faculty Development Grants and the Henry Luce III Fund for Distinguished Scholarship.

1. I have changed the name of this retirement community at their request. The general manager of the retirement community at the time of my research suggested "The Heritage" as a suitable name. All the names of the women I interviewed and the names of those people who appear in the women's stories have been changed as well.

References Cited

Abu-Lughod, Lila. 1993. *Writing Women's Worlds: Bedouin Stories*. Berkeley: University of California Press.

Alt, Betty Sowers and Bonnie Domrose Stone. 1991. *Campfollowing: A History of the Military Wife*. New York: Praeger.

Baker, Alison. 1998. *Voices of Resistance: Oral Histories of Moroccan Women*. New York: SUNY Press.

Behar, Ruth. 1993. *Translated Woman: Crossing the Border with Esperanza's Story*. Boston: Beacon Press.

Collins, Randall. 1992. "Women and the Production of Status Cultures." In *Cultivating Differences: Symbolic Boundaries and the Making of Inequality*, Michele Lamont and Marcel Fournier, eds. Pp. 213–231. Chicago: The University of Chicago Press.

Coontz, Stephanie. 1992. *The Way We Never Were: American Families and the Nostalgia Trap*. New York, NY: Basic Books.

Daniels, Arlene K. 1988. *Invisible Careers: Women Civic Leaders from the Volunteer World*. Chicago: The University of Chicago Press.

di Leonardo, Michela, 1992. "The Female World of Cards and Holidays: Women, Families and the Work of Kinship." In *Rethinking The Family*. Thorne and Yalom, eds. Pp. 247–261. Boston: Northeastern Universal Press.

Patai, Daphne. 1988. *Brazilian Women Speak: Contemporary Life Stories*. New Brunswick, NJ: Rutgers University Press.

Prieto, Norma Iglesias. 1997. *Beautiful Flowers of the Maquiladora: Life Histories of Women Workers in Tijuana*. Michael Stone with Gabrielle Winkler, trans. Austin: University of Texas Press.

Randall, Margaret. 1994. *Sandino's Daughters Revisited: Feminism in Nicaragua*. New Brunswick, NJ: Rutgers University Press.

———. 1995 [1981]. *Sandino's Daughters: Testimonies of Nicaraguan Women in Struggle*. New Brunswick, NJ: Rutgers University Press.

Scott, Kesho Yvonne. 1991. *The Habit of Surviving: Black Women's Strategies for Life*. New Brunswick, NJ: Rutgers University Press.

Shea, Nancy. 1966 [1941]. *The Army Wife*. revised by Anna Perle Smith. 4th edition. New York: Harper & Row.

CHAPTER 4

Gender- and Class-Based Role Expectations for Army Spouses

Margaret C. Harrell

T his chapter stems from previous academic research on the expectations for Army spouses. That work asserted a relationship between class identity and the expected gender-based roles for Army spouses, based on interviews with over one hundred military spouses of all ranks, as well as with military soldiers and other professionals who deal with issues relating to military families.[1] This paper further addresses the extent to which class-based identities shape the role expectations and perceptions for Army spouses.[2]

This work asserts that the expectations for spouses are culturally gendered roles that are different for officers' wives and for junior enlisted wives and that these differences have generally paralleled the nation's social class barriers. In other words, the perceptions of and role expectations for Army spouses result from their class associations. To address these points, I discuss the meaning of gendered roles, then progress through a brief history of Army spouses, and then discuss current expectations for and perceptions of Army spouses. I then evaluate the extent to which gendered role expectations continue to reflect class association in the military community before concluding with assertions about what today's stereotypes and role expectations say about social progress in the Army.

Spouse Roles are Culturally Gendered

It is important to establish that spouse roles in the Army are culturally constructed roles for women: These are the roles of Army wives. There are several elements to this point. First, male spouses are not expected to perform these roles (thus they are gendered), and second, there is no biological reason why men cannot perform these roles (and thus they are culturally gendered).

Previous work had found that male spouses of female officers were not expected to satisfy the same roles as their female counterparts (Bourg 1995) and that male spouses were even excluded from gatherings of spouses. My research had similar findings. When male spouses choose to attend Officer Spouse Club (OSC) functions or to be active in their wife's unit, they are met with a mixture of curiosity, delight, amusement, and resistance, but no one assumes or demands their participation. Some wives welcome, but still do not assume, male spouse participation. As one senior officer's wife said: "I'm happy to have male spouses. Most of them are nonparticipating. It's just not a comfort zone for a lot of men to come to the spouses' clubs or the coffees. But once in a while you'll have one that comes and he's a great sport, you know. It definitely broadens the views in the group. And I certainly am capable of talking about things other than mommy things."

However, many male spouses report difficulty trying to fill the role, as they are often excluded from activities and must be ever conscious of negative appearances and innuendo by avoiding instances that would place them alone with a female spouse.

The data clearly support the finding that men are not expected to fill the Army spouse role. It is also possible to prove that the role is culturally constructed; there is nothing that would prevent men from filling the role of officer's spouse. The social aspects, the cooking and cleaning, the administrative work, fund raising, and so on (described later), are all things that are done professionally by some men. Indeed, the world's most accomplished chefs are predominantly male. Additionally, anthropological literature provides rich examples of societies in which men have filled the role of military "wife" and thus underscore the lack of biological factors that would preclude men from filling this role in our culture. Perhaps the best-known case is that of the Azande (Evans-Pritchard 1970 and 1971; Murray and Roscoe 1998).

A Brief History of Army Wives

Historically, marriage has been central to the military's ideal characterization of an officer, and the absence of marriage has been equally central to the definition of an enlisted soldier. Not surprisingly, the history of officers, enlisted men, and their spouses dramatically reflect this difference. Officers and their spouses have occupied a very different position from that of enlisted men and their spouses. This separateness is evident in the United States from the pre–Civil War period onward. By presenting an appropriate picture of domestic success, responsible procreation (only through marriage), and social expertise, the officer's wife traditionally has been proof of maturity as well as the social and sexual control that was perceived to define an Army officer. In contrast, throughout history the military leadership has repeatedly prohibited, expelled, or simply disregarded enlisted spouses. Unlike the public demonstrations of domestic success historically evident in the entertaining lifestyle of officers, the private lives of enlisted soldiers were neither visible nor endorsed by the Army. Instead, enlisted soldiers have been treated as if they were adolescents, or less than adults, and thus not expected to have families or responsible social lives.

The available historical material about nineteenth-century military wives consists mostly of the letters, diaries, and memoirs of officers' wives, who were encouraged to keep diaries (Crossley and Keller 1993:xxiii). Because many enlisted wives were illiterate, and others did not have the domestic assistance that would have permitted them the luxury to record their memoirs, or perhaps because they did not have the financial means to preserve and publish their writings, the information available is very lopsided.

While we are unable to draw firsthand information about the lives and experiences of enlisted wives, we do have information about the ways in which these women were perceived by, and interacted with, officers' wives. This information sketches a picture of two groups of white women, both of whom were limited by strict gender roles. However, these roles and, indeed, the women themselves were separated from one another because of the military separation of officers and enlisted men. This separation designated categories of women who were expected to, or precluded from, doing certain things, the most notable of which was marrying, keeping a house, and raising a family. These activities were clearly expected of officers' wives and discouraged among enlisted wives.

In the peacetime immediately prior to the Civil War, "[e]nlisted men had an unenviable place in American society. . . . The best a soldier could hope for was that his fellow Americans would ignore him, and most did. When he attracted comment, he became an object of contempt and fear. It could be argued that commentators held similar views generally of immigrants and laborers, the classes from which most men in the ranks came. But the man who enlisted incurred added opprobrium because he not only opted out of the competitive economic system but, worse still, he also voluntarily gave up rights civilians enjoyed" (Coffman 1986:137).

As this passage demonstrates, the enlisted soldier was clearly perceived of negatively and as similar to (or worse than) lower-class civilian men. Indeed, enlisted personnel suffered even more negative perceptions than did their peers who chose not to enter the military. This class orientation was shared by and reflected on the women who married these men and thereby shared their less-than-positive reputation. However, these women were largely ignored.

The military alternatively used and discarded the wives of enlisted soldiers. Often referred to as camp followers, they were considered the nemesis of many military commanders trying to feed and maintain a ready force at remote frontier locations with limited resources. As a result, the military worked to control their numbers. As early as 1803 there appeared a general order which forbade "loose females . . . in camp or quarters" and specified that only "the regular allowance of married women of good conduct are to be permitted to the Companies" (Coffman 1986:25). Thus, when the wives of the enlisted men struggled to establish homes for their husbands and families in shanties or abandoned buildings, they were at the mercy of the commander, who could order them to leave. The negative connotations associated with these camp followers is evident in the term "shacking up," which survives to describe a questionable domestic arrangement, but originated with the laundresses who augmented their incomes by providing sexual services in the shanties outside the military garrison (Little 1971:248), and in the term "hooker," which is rumored to come from the Civil War camp followers of General Joseph Hooker's men.

That the order referred to "loose females" takes on additional significance when one considers that the military commander actually controlled which of these women married soldiers or were just living with them. Thus the commander could determine who and how many women were morally questionable or "loose," while also dictating which women were to be excluded from the garrison. Indeed, enlisted personnel were required to obtain official permission to marry, and many officers discouraged marriage among the enlisted ranks: "Colonel Simonds of the Sixth Infantry informed his command in 1811 that any soldier contemplating that serious step must have the approval of his company commander, 'as the Regiment seems to be threatened from a spirit of matrimony, with so great an abundance of engagements as to become injurious to the Service'" (Coffman 1986:25). At other times, the military banned the enlistment of married men in order to limit the number of camp followers.

The military treated officers' wives significantly differently, although life as an officer's wife was still not an easy life. While the military did not deny officers the right to marry, officers generally were dissuaded from marrying until the age of thirty to thirty-five. This was generally accepted for financial reasons, as junior officers were not remunerated to support a family. Those women who did marry officers accepted a life of "glittering misery" (Summerhayes 1911:235). The Army made few provisions for the officer's family, and the frequent moves were just one costly aspect of military life. An 1836 *Army Navy Chronicle* article (quoted by Coffman 1986:117) described the financial difficulties these limits entailed when it reported that the moves "prove oppressive to the extreme, and often keep them [officers with families] on the verge of destitution."

Similarly, Martha Summerhayes describes the constraints she faced: She could move all of her belongings that fit into three trunks, and these trunks repeatedly suffered such misfortune as being dumped in rivers (Summerhayes 1911). These limitations and hardships resulted both in expensive moves and very simple living conditions. The more junior the officer, the more likely that both the move would be expensive and the living conditions meager, making the lower officer ranks less conducive to marriage and family life.

Once married, the hard realities of military life left these women with few romantic sentiments. In general, their lives were considerably more difficult than the civilian life most had left behind, and some bases were more primitive than others. Even when their accommodations were sufficient, however, the remoteness of the military lifestyle sometimes meant that only four or five officers resided at a post. If the other officers were unmarried, these women would suffer from months of loneliness and limit their socializing to the male officers rather than interact socially with the enlisted wives (Coffman 1986:292).

This separation applied also to other women in the military community, specifically officers' mistresses. As the acting commander of the Third Infantry in 1843 explained to a lieutenant who wanted to take a woman of "unsavory reputation" with him when the regiment moved, "such behavior would not only lead to his personal ruin, but also, if all officers did as he, to the destruction of the regiment" (Coffman 1986:108). Presumably, this "destruction" would be the result of "unsavory" women replacing chaste officers' wives. This view asserts the need the military felt for the proper wife, as well as the military's desire to control the men's marriages and sexual liaisons. These attitudes also indicate that the military defined the proper woman, and officer's wife, as an upper-class white woman.

The class and gender structure of the nineteenth century both defined and divided women in the military community. Officers' wives were a distinct group of women held separate from the other groups: enlisted men's wives and mistresses of officers or enlisted men. Membership in any of the other groups precluded a woman from ever being accepted as an officer's wife. The military both constructed these roles and kept women within them. For example, by refusing permission for marriage, the military kept women from marrying enlisted men, thus retaining them in the role of mistresses and unofficial camp followers. Even among officers' wives, there was a strict delineation of rank and prestige, embodied by the practice of "falling bricks," whereby an officer and his wife were evicted from their home anytime a more senior married officer arrived. They, in turn, evicted the next junior couple, and onward down the line.

In the 1900s, more officers began marrying at a younger age, and their wives began to fill a more defining class-associated role. Relatively few West Point graduates came from upper-class or upper working-class families.[3] For these officers, marrying the upper-class white socialites recruited from northeastern society to attend academy social events was not only convenient, it was class-securing: "This system served to maintain the social and regional exclusiveness of the military profession, and. . . . marriage on the basis of academy ties was a validation of status aspirations" (Janowitz 1960:190). Thus, the very selection of certain women for wives defined the status of the male officers as upper class. As the following comment from a historical account of officers indicates, the existence of a proper wife was perceived as critical to the success of an officer: "To be without a wife was a real career handicap, and a grave inconvenience in the circumscribed life of the military community where family and professional relations were intertwined. If a first marriage was terminated because of the death of the partner or because of personal discord, remarriage was essential and often arranged" (Janowitz 1960:190). Indeed, this necessity was so acknowledged that the military community interacted with upper-class families specifically to arrange an appropriate marriage for an officer.

Because the military community was concerned almost solely with officers' family life, activities were centered around the "patterns of gentlemanly conduct associated with the officer corps" (Little 1971:248). During the early 1900s, the military became a more pleasant institution for officers' families and adopted many of the social aspects of upper-class civilians. Officers' clubs with swimming pools and tennis courts were built, and polo and horseback riding were available for Army officers and dependents, while those on Navy bases enjoyed yachting and boating. These pleasures also included active socializing with upper-class civilians (Janowitz 1971:176, 184). Pamela Frese has presented this world in more detail in chapter 3.

The 1920s and 1930s were a time when social protocol was increasingly important: "It was a time of calling cards and engraved invitations to afternoon teas, gala balls, and elaborate receptions. . . . The success of an officer's career was closely linked to his wife's ability to entertain" (Alt and Stone 1991:85) and being able to entertain with grace and style indicated an upper-class family background. Thus, successful participation in these social events was further evidence of the high status of both an officer and his wife.

In addition, officers' wives were expected to be active in volunteer activities, and they raised funds for the Red Cross and the Army and Navy League (Crossley and Keller 1993:xxv). These expectations are consistent with traditional upper-class participation in charity and volunteer activities in the civilian community, where "upper-class wives in particular spen[t] a great deal of time on boards of charitable organizations, in fund-raising" (Collins 1992). Charity organizations in the civilian world brought together women of similar class ranking, which increased the elite-factor of the activity and also tightened the class boundaries between those upper-class women who participated and lower-class women who could not afford the luxury of participating in uncompensated labor.

Cultural anthropology permits the observation that this volunteerism also served as a form of status production (Collins 1992). In his analysis of gift-giving, Mauss described that whenever a gift cannot be returned, the status of the giver is increased ([1950] 1990).[4] Collins builds from Mauss's work to assert that charity participation "is perhaps the purest form of conversion of wealth into status" because the poor who are assisted by the charity efforts are unable to recompense the wealthy (Collins 1992:226). Thus, through their group participation in charity organizations, officers' wives were both defining the class boundaries of the officer community and also securing the officers' high status. Class and status were evident both in the availability of these women to perform volunteerism (only upper-class families can afford the domestic assistance to release the wives to volunteerism) as well as from the social transactions themselves.

Meanwhile, the enlisted men and their wives of the early twentieth century lived very separate lives from those of officers and their families. In the early decades of the 1900s, few enlisted men were married. At the time of World War I, being married was even a way to avoid military service: Of the 4,883,213 married men who registered with the draft board, over 74 percent of them were deferred (Alt and Stone 1991:76). In 1925 the War Department began to permit enlisted men to marry, although these men still needed the permission of their superior officer. The restrictions stated that "marriage must be for some good reason in the public interest," and "the efficiency of the service is to be the first consideration" (Crossley and Keller 1993:xxv). Officially, Army enlisted personnel still require permission from senior personnel to marry, although this has not been uniformly enforced since the early 1980s.[5]

Despite these limitations, the population of married enlisted men grew considerably, and the 1930s saw large numbers of these enlisted families living in extremely squalid conditions very different from the accommodations of officers and their families. The living conditions were so bad that some commanders repaired abandoned buildings and made them available for these families (Alt and Stone 1991:84). The Army Chief of Staff grew concerned that enlisted men were marrying and having families on enlisted pay, which was not sufficient (or intended to be sufficient) to support a family (ibid.). In 1942, Congress finally passed the Serviceman's Dependents Allowance Act, which officially noted the presence of enlisted families by augmenting the pay of enlisted men with dependents. However, this monetary recognition would come and go.[6]

Enlisted families remained virtually invisible to the officers' community, and although the children of enlisted personnel were schooled on Army bases, the military schools of this period were segregated—enlisted children did not attend class with officers' children (Janowitz 1960:180).[7]

In summary, class and status barriers between the enlisted community and the officer community date to the early years of the U.S. Army. These barriers translated into very different experiences for the two communities of women. While the lives of enlisted spouses were consistent with those of working spouses in the civilian community, the upper-class origin of Army officers' wives and the need to maintain the upper-class status of Army officers dictated the behaviors and roles of officers' wives.

Current Expected Roles for, and Perceptions of, Officers' Wives[8]

Generations of memoirs by, and handbooks for, officers' spouses detail the extensive role expectations for women married to officers (See for example, handbooks by Cline 1995; Crossley and Keller 1993; Gross 1980; Kinzer and Leach 1966; Murphy and Parker 1966; Shea 1954, 1966; and articles and memoirs by Clark 1956; Combs 1981; Garrett 1986; Gibbons 1984; Lane 1987; Marshall 1946; Riley 1988.) Nonetheless, more recent research by Durand (1995) asserts that while wives exhibit an attitudinal commitment to the military, they do not necessarily translate this into behavior. Weinstein and Mederer (1997) report that submarine officers' wives do participate in a "two-person career" framework, but that these women view this behavior as "choice" rather than "sacrifice." This is all consistent with official guidance in the late 1980s that acknowledged the right of officers' spouses to pursue their own interests. Thus, one might expect to find an Army more accommodating to social change, cognizant and consistent with social realities, such as women with career interests and the need for double incomes in families.

There is a relative paucity of material regarding the expected roles of enlisted spouses. Rosenberg (1989) conducted semistructured personal interviews with the wives of first-term enlisted soldiers and concluded that most did not have any clearly defined perception of an expected role. While relatively limited in that it only addressed spouses of very junior enlisted personnel, Rosenberg's work provided a valuable basis for research.

To understand the expected roles for officers' spouses and enlisted spouses, it is important to acknowledge that today's Army is a compelling mix of the past, present, and future. The past is relived daily in the tradition and ceremony still apparent throughout the daily activities on an Army post, beginning with the bugler's reveille and concluding with the evening flag ceremony. "Change of Command" and other ceremonies still recall the Army of the nineteenth century. However, realities of the present and the future are inescapable for the Army. Societal changes have compelled the Army to face new manpower and personnel issues: female military personnel, dual-career couples, increasing numbers of married enlisted soldiers, single parents, and spouses with their own career aspirations. Additionally, emerging missions have created an Army in which certain kinds of units are frequently deployed, adding to the personal stress faced by these personnel and their families. These changes all arrived in an environment of budgetary pressures where there are constrained resources to support any resulting problems. The expected roles for spouses are tied very closely to this combination of demographic change, emerging missions, and constrained resources.

Current Role Expectations for Officers' Spouses

The expected role for officers' spouses is largely based on volunteerism. At first glance this seems not much different from the roles expected of white-gloved officers' wives from decades past, however, closer examination indicates both similarities and differences. The activities expected of officers' spouses can be categorized into: institutional activities; morale, public relations and ceremonial duties; mentoring, development, and role preservation; entertaining and socializing; and unit and readiness support. The extent to which spouses are expected and feel compelled to participate vary by category as well as by the officer's job.

Institutional activities include volunteerism to support organizations ranging from the Red Cross and Girl Scouts to agencies within the military community (Army Family Team Building, Army Community Services, the post library, etc.) as well as seasonal activities, such as Toys for Tots. Volunteerism in formal organizations, especially the Red Cross, has traditionally been a part of the role of an officer's wife. Currently, this kind of volunteerism is not perceived to be compelled. Generally, individuals who support these organizations do so for their own personal satisfaction or to gain work experience.

Morale, public relations, and ceremonial duties are also a traditional category of activities for officers' spouses and are related to the fact that an officer's wife becomes an extension of the officer. All spouses are compelled to participate at the most minimal level of representing their husband, obeying military rules and laws, and being presentable and appropriate at all times in the military community. However, for wives whose husbands are in command, this role becomes more extensive, and includes such occasions as the ceremonial change of command, where the incoming commander's spouse is presented with a bouquet of roses.

Mentoring, development, and role preservation activities include efforts by senior spouses to mentor and teach younger or more junior spouses about the expectations they will encounter. While many senior spouses recall being firmly guided by the "Old Army" wives, today's mentoring generally is done with a softer hand. Nonetheless, there are still senior spouses who pronounce to other spouses, as did the general's wife at one location: "I don't work anymore. I quit my job; I just do the 'wifey' thing. And you know, I'm going to do the 'wifey' thing the whole time I'm here, and I expect you to do the 'wifey' thing with me."

Entertaining and socializing activities consist of a large portion of the current expectations for the spouses of officers in command. The socializing includes unit-related functions (hail and farewells, balls, and spouse coffees) and peer-attended functions, such as monthly dinners attended by all commanders or monthly meetings for senior commanders' spouses. The combination of these functions can easily consume a calendar. These functions also can result in considerable financial stress, given the cost of hosting functions, dressing appropriately for occasions, and hiring baby-sitters.[9]

Many of the spouses spoke positively of the opportunities to socialize, but most grew weary of the events, and most also acknowledged that they often had little choice but to participate. The following comment reveals the extent to which these events are mandated for many commanders and their spouses:

> Once a month, normally once a month, we have [a commanders' dinner]. And that's on a rotating basis. And there are about 40 people involved in that. And it's a social thing. It used to be a dinner. Now it's heavy hors d'oeuvres. We used to do sit-down dinners for forty people, if you can imagine. . . . It's a wonderful evening, but it's very, very hard to do. [Now] it's better, but it's still a lot of work. . . . It's the chief of staff. It's the two [assistant division commanders]. It's the command sergeant major. And it's all the O-6s [colonels] and their wives. . . . The chief of staff calls my husband and says, "Can you do it? It's your turn." And he says, "Yep, we can do it." They give us the date, and we do it.

Similarly, one battalion commander's wife speaks of the monthly dinners for all the command personnel within the brigade:

> [The new brigade commander] invited us all over for dinner. So we're all over there having a really nice time. The end of the dinner comes. . . . He said, "This is what we're going to do. Every month one of you will host a dinner." He had a calendar. Every month—he already had us programmed into what month. . . . All these people come. All the high-ranking command sergeant majors. Battalion commanders and their spouses. It'd be about sixteen people if everybody came. [And they usually do,] because if you blow it off, I mean, you have to have a good reason why you're not there. There's nothing in writing, but you know how it is. This is something I'm supposed to go to every month.

The importance of socializing is perhaps best captured by the comments of one colonel's spouse who explained that one of the brigade commanders at her location referred to colonels' spouses as "the DUSUAN (pronounced Doo-Shwan) Society. That stands for Dress Up, Show Up, and Act Nice, and he was saying that as commanders' spouses, as O-6 spouses, that's what our function is, to dress up, show up, and act nice."

Unit and readiness support represents the newest kind of activities for officers' spouses and often the most substantial share of their activities. This category includes the maintenance of a healthy Family Support Group (FSG), which is described below in more detail.[10] This category of activity applies only to the commanders' spouses, but it is generally the most time-consuming activity expected of officers' spouses. This is also the activity most likely to reflect directly on the officer. Spouse participation in or resistance to some of the activities described above could impact a senior officer's view of a particular officer and thus potentially impact that officer's future opportunities. Officers are evaluated on the health of their Family Support Group. Although the official directives and training materials assert that a commander's spouse need not participate in this activity, the reality is that—absent an enthusiastic volunteer—the responsibility falls to the commander's spouse. While the intent of this chapter is not to evaluate fully the system, it is important to understand the kinds of tasks the FSG does, in order to understand the magnitude of responsibility that falls on the commander's spouse. Thus, the following attempts to briefly explain the FSG system.

The Army states that "basic FSG goals include supporting the military mission through provision of support, outreach, and information to family members" (U.S. Army 1993a:1). The regulation states "Unit FSGs are a command sponsored vehicle for people within the unit to help each other. FSGs provide a communication network to pass information to families, and a conduit to identify problems or needs to the command. In addition to communication and family activities, FSGs create a unique atmosphere of mutual care and concern among unit families. FSG groups also become a vital link between families, the [Rear Detachment], the soldiers and community agencies during mobilization and deployments" (United States Army 1993a:2).

The official Army materials translate the responsibilities of FSGs into a list of essential activities, such as holding meetings, publishing a newsletter and maintaining telephone rosters; and typical activities, such as sponsoring new families, orienting newcomers, organizing holiday parties, compiling lists of child care and even providing short-term care, arranging transportation for unit spouses, providing stress management workshops, planning homecoming activities, and raising funds (United States Army 1993a,b).

The essential and typical activities make up a daunting list; many could consume an individual full time. The commander's spouse who is enthused about this role finds herself with a full slate of activities, one who does not want this responsibility generally finds herself overwhelmed by compulsory activities. My interviews indicates that she often feels coerced into the role, given the importance of the FSG to her husband's career and the dearth of volunteers to lead the group. A company commander's wife explains:

[When my husband became company commander, I] took a one-day training course and [the general's wife] came and spoke to us. . . . And one of the things that's assumed is that the officers' wives are going to run the Family Support Group, and sometimes that's not always the best person to run it. You have the first sergeants' wives that have been in there sixteen, seventeen years that are quite capable. But it is assumed that the officer's wife is going to run it. You can step back, but then people speculate, you know, make up other reasons as to why you're not doing it. Like you don't support your husband. You don't support the military. Things like that. Which they haven't said about me yet. I haven't given them a chance. But I hear it among the wives.

In summary, officers' wives today still encounter role expectations. While these expectations are negligible for the many who are not married to commanders, they are more considerable than ever for commanders' wives. The level of commitment required by commanders' spouses has increased in the 1990s, since the institution of FSGs. Leading the FSG is new and different from any of the previous role expectations for officers' spouses for two reasons: First, managing the FSG directly impacts the military workplace and the evaluated performance of the commander. Second, leading the FSG requires officers' wives to develop relationships with the enlisted spouses and families to an extent that was not required previously. The characteristics of these responsibilities are very relevant to the relationship between class and the expected roles.

Perceptions of Officers' Wives

The existence of some class identity is still evident in the perceptions of officers' wives and the separation experienced between officers and enlisted wives.[11] While many spouses of noncommissioned officers (NCO)[12] have friends who are officers' wives, they typically spoke of their friendships as either exceptional or as relatively limited. Either they were exceptional in that their friend was untypical (i.e., all officers' wives are snotty—except for my friend) or they acknowledged that they could not freely associate with their friend and include their soldier spouses. In these cases, the spouses enjoyed one another's company, but their friendship was often limited to one another, exclusive of their soldier spouses. If they did socialize as couples, then they were limited to out-of-the-way locations or to their private homes. The main exceptions to these perceived limitations were when officers and NCOs with closely related jobs socialized together (e.g., company commanders and first sergeants).

The existence of class separation of officers' spouses is also evident in the negative perception of officers' spouses. While many women commented on exceptions to the rule, such a negative perception of perceived superiority does exist. It is notable that this perception is often handed down or taught to junior enlisted spouses by NCO spouses:

> The sergeant's wife said, well, you could tell she was an officer's wife because of the attitude that she had. It's like they are better than enlisted folk, but I don't know. I couldn't really say. I should hope that is not true.
>
> —Junior enlisted spouse

> My coworker has an uppity attitude because her husband is the commander. "He's this. He went to college all these years. He has his degree." Fine. But it couldn't be that great if he's in the military. That's my motto. Because if he got his doctorate in yadda, yadda, yadda, why isn't he making all this money doing yadda, yadda, yadda. Why is he in the Army?
>
> —NCO spouse

> My sister's husband retired as a colonel, so I always saw her as the epitome of being a colonel's wife. Kind of stuck up and snooty. But the colonels' wives that I knew were not like that. There are exceptions.
>
> —NCO spouse

> Most of the officers' wives think they are better than the enlisted wives. I guess because they get more money and they live in better housing and they get this and that. They just think they are better, which makes me mad, and then they put you down because you are an enlisted member's wife.
>
> —Junior enlisted spouse

> I've been told that some could be stuck up. I rode with these two other enlisted wives, and I was talking about how I had lost my wallet, but I found it, and she was saying that she had found a wallet in the Wal-Mart parking lot and it happened to belong to a major's wife, and it had like $200 and something dollars in it. She hadn't opened it and looked for the money. She just noticed that it had a military ID and gave it to the MPs. That lady never even called and said thank you or nothing. [My friend] said that if it had been a private's wife, she would have probably called. I think that's true, too. To a private, $200 is a lot more than to a major, because they got all the money.
>
> —Junior enlisted spouse

I work with a couple of officers' spouses. They think they know everything. That they have this great crystal ball that has the answers to everything. And they have no clue.

—NCO spouse

Some officers' wives do maintain a social distance from the enlisted community for reasons they believe valid. In some instances, the barrier is based on the traditional social exclusion of enlisted spouses and the class difference between the communities. It is in this context that officers' spouses will explain to the more junior officers' spouses "We don't need to associate with the enlisted spouses. That's just not the way it works."

Other wives use the fraternization policy[13] as an acceptable reason why they should not associate across the officer/enlisted boundary. From a commander's spouse: "In another life, I think she and I would be best friends, and it is not that we are not good friends here, but there is that barrier between us." Many spouses defend this separation as completely necessary and based on the military mission. One senior officer's wife explains the need for this separation: "If you get to know and have family friends with these people [the enlisted force], and then you go into battle and you've got to send somebody out for the point job, who are you going to send? The one that comes over and you know as a friend? You know their children and their wives. How can you make this judgment call of who to send out there, possibly to get killed?"

There is validity to this explanation when applied to junior officers, the enlisted people they command, and the spouses of each. Junior officers are more likely to have to send enlisted personnel into direct harm's way, and the decision of whom to send might be muddled by the knowledge that your spouses are close friends. This is certainly one reason why the fraternization rules just quoted exist, even though the rules do not apply directly to the spouses. However, the spouse speaking above and many others adopt this logic and the fraternization rules as a convenient justification for the separation and distancing between spouses. One problem with this logic, however, is that it ignores the reality that senior officers may make decisions that endanger the lives of particular junior officers, by deciding which unit gets sent in harm's way or on a risky mission. Yet there are no limitations between close mentoring relationships of senior officers and junior officers, or of their respective spouses. Nonetheless, it is more comfortable for the quoted spouse (and others) to remain removed from "these people," and the fraternization policy is a convenient justification. Some officers and their spouses appear to regret the division and explain that there are particular enlisted personnel or enlisted spouses (generally from the NCO community) with whom they would be friendly, but they are conscious of the chain of command and the potential for perceived abuse of position.

In many situations, it is the enlisted wives who maintain the social barrier. This is likely related to the negative "schooling" they have received regarding "snooty" officers' wives. The result is a "ma'am barrier" that serves as an effective screen between the two communities. One officer's spouse expresses frustration that even established relationships fall prey to the ma'am barrier:

[My daughter] Karen was in third grade last year and met this little girl. She would come over to our house and Karen went over to her house and played. And I would talk to her mom all the time. And I was always very elusive as to what Cliff's job was. I would just say, "He's with the battalion." When she realized that he was the battalion commander, I became "ma'am." And I said, "We've known each other for four months. We've talked at school. We've gone on field trips. We've done all these things. It's 'Susan,' it's not 'ma'am.'" But it was like "bam." It was instantly there. Even after you felt like you had that relationship built up a little, all of a sudden it was "ma'am" again.

In summary, there does exist a negative stereotype of officers' spouses as "snooty" and superior. This stereotype was not universally supported. However, I interviewed junior enlisted spouses who had not met an officer's wife, but had heard of the negative characteristics of this group of women, with "snootiness" the most widely acknowledged characteristic. Most of the NCO spouses were friendly with at least some officers' wives, but they regarded their friends as the exception to the rule. These NCO wives will assert that other officers' wives—not their friends—were snooty and aloof and not well informed as to the real problems in the enlisted community. These negative perceptions are consistent with parallel situations of civilian social class. For example, blue-collar workers perceive their managers and those of social classes above to be snooty, self-elevating, and not knowledgeable about the "real" world and "real" work (See, for example, Ortner 1991). The class-based separation of officers' wives from other wives in the military community is still present, and while this separation is not supported by all military spouses, it is maintained by some from both sides of the barrier.

Current Expected Roles for, and Perceptions of, Junior Enlisted Wives

Consistent with Rosenberg's prior research (1989), this work did not find proactive role expectations for junior enlisted spouses. To the contrary, the role expectations are negative and passive. The ideal junior enlisted spouse is one who does not present difficulties, either for the soldier or for the soldier's unit. These spouses are not expected to be active in the military community and are in fact isolated from that community in several ways. Junior enlisted couples are often less likely to receive military housing, which isolates them geographically from the military community. Soldiers also actively isolate their spouses from their units and from supportive opportunities within the community. Notices of events or facilities that are sent home via junior enlisted soldiers tend not to reach their spouses, report FSG leaders, company commanders, and others who have attempted such communications. My research also indicated that junior enlisted spouses were not informed, that young soldiers did not share information about the military with their spouse. While unfortunate, the soldiers' motivation is clear: Their wives cannot help them by becoming involved with the unit. Junior soldiers are not evaluated positively because their wives are active in the unit or the military community. However, if their wives are perceived to be a nuisance to the unit or speak out of turn to the unit leadership, then soldiers can bear the brunt of this misfortune. Retribution reportedly can range from harassment, such as extra duty, to reduced likelihood for advancement or for unique opportunities within the unit. The allocation of harassment or positive opportunities is often extremely subjective, and the annoyance factor can play a strong role in such decisions. Thus, soldiers prefer to maintain separation between their wives and the military.

The ideal role of a junior enlisted spouse is to be invisible but sufficiently capable to avoid causing problems. What is generally perceived of junior enlisted spouses, however, is not that they fulfill the ideal role, but instead that they embody a tremendously negative class-based stereotype, that junior enlisted are unintelligent, uneducated, immoral kids. Explanations such as this by a junior enlisted soldier talking about his own peer group were very typical: "A lot of the E-1 to E-4 people are total idiots. They're here because they had nowhere else to go.... They are pretty much the losers in high school." Similarly, an NCO's spouse comments on the Army's role in addressing the moral shortcomings of soldiers: "My husband says that the biggest thing he sees nowadays with young soldiers coming in is that they have no values and no morals. And [the Army] is having to instill these things in these young men, which they should have learned at home."

The youth and perceived immorality of junior enlisted soldiers is perceived to preclude the possibility of a strong marriage, and their unstable marriages pose a direct contrast to the "perfect" and controlled home lives of officers. Even junior enlisted personnel speak negatively of other junior enlisted marriages, as is evident in the following comments where the couples are characterized as immature, promiscuous, or marrying for reasons of greed: "Even though I'm his wife, and I'm married and stuff, I don't feel that I get as much respect as . . . an officer's wife would. You know, because sometimes, a lot of times, like the military guys just get married or whatever. And the girl might just want his benefits or his money or whatever. Some people don't know our history together, so they just think that . . . . have never cheated on him. But they just assume that 'you're young, it's not going to last' or things like that. . . . There are a lot of girls around an Army base that are like that."

The debate of whether or not junior enlisted families should have children is frequent and ongoing: "You've got 18- and 19-year-olds who can't get a job anyplace else, that have three kids . . . those are the people who cause the trouble"; "To be married and a private is ridiculous . . . and they are having babies! What are they thinking?"

The willingness of those interviewed to express an opinion about junior enlisted personnel and their personal, family decisions seemed also to make a class statement: The personal lives of the enlisted community were open to censure and comment from anyone who perceived themselves superior in intelligence, judgment, or capability. The stereotype of junior enlisted couples also included negative perceptions about their general ability to maintain a home for their children. This presumption is consistent with civilian assumptions and observations about lower-class couples: They tend to be characterized by others as bad parents and atrocious housekeepers. In general, their domestic skills are thoroughly demeaned, with common references to filth, dirt, slum living, unacceptable personal hygiene, inappropriate dressing, slovenly behavior, and greedy eating. These perceptions all reaffirm junior enlisted couples as lower class in contrast to the high values placed on cleanliness, respectability, and presentability in middle- and upper-class circles. Even those who believe they are championing the case of junior enlisted spouses often reiterate the stereotypes, as is as evident in the following comment by an NCO's spouse: "I don't care if you are the general's spouse. If you are attending this function, and you want this private's wife to attend, why shouldn't she be able to attend? All you need to do is teach her how to dress and how to have a little manners." Once again, the evident perception is that they lack manners or basic knowledge of how to dress. Thus, there is a widely held class-based stereotype of junior enlisted personnel and their spouses as immature, immoral, freely reproductive couples with few social graces or redeeming features.

The notion of reforming these spouses has been institutionalized in a formal handbook, *Mrs. NCO*, first published in 1969 and revised and reprinted in 1980.[14] This book attempts to train NCO spouses to be presentable women with basic social skills, given the increased likelihood that as NCO wives they will be more active in, and less isolated from, the military community. The contents of the book clearly indicate an assumption that enlisted spouses are lower class and lacking in the social polish necessary to prepare them for their new roles as NCO wives. For example, the beginning of the book includes questions and answers regarding social situations. Some of the questions and answers are posed such that none of the alternatives the new NCO spouse asks about are even vaguely acceptable:

> Q. In order to reserve a seat at a Wives' Club luncheon should I place my bag on the table, or tilt the chair forward?
> A. To do either is the height of rudeness. If reservations are to be made, get in touch with the hostess. (Gross 1980:9)
>
> Q. Is it permissible to put my cup and saucer on the tea table when I am through?
> A. Heavens no! The hostess has given much care to see that she has a lovely table and certainly would not appreciate your ruining its appearance with your soiled cup and saucer. (Gross 1980:20)

The contents of this handbook also include detailed social guidelines for negotiating everything from seating plans to menus. One such set of guidelines provided is a pronunciation and word choice guide and the French terms needed to negotiate many menus. This is shown in figure 4.1.

An examination of the contents of these materials underscores the class differentiation, as the lists implies that a new NCO wife would be so socially rough and inept that she would not know that *à la king* is pronounced "ah lah king" and that she would not have had the benefit of either French lessons or travel to French-speaking countries. Further, this stereotypical former enlisted spouse also would be inclined to speak of "EYE-talions" rather than "eh-TALIONS," might call the "PO-lice" before requesting the assistance of the "pu-LEECE," and might not know how to conjugate verbs correctly. These kinds of errors are addressed in a second set of guidelines, shown here as figure 4.2.

Conclusion

The role expectations for Army spouses are culturally gendered, and these roles differ for officers' wives and for junior enlisted wives. Officers' wives

Don't Say	Say Instead
old antique	antique, all antiques are old
lousy	unpleasant, mean, bad
semi-formal	formal or informal
sack	bed
chow	dinner
an invite	invitation
Daddy (meaning husband)	Bob—my husband
stink	smell bad or unpleasant odor
shut up	hush or be quiet
swell	good
Where is it at?	Where is it?
Pleased to meet you.	How do you do, or Hello
EYE-talion	eh-TALION
LI-berry	li-BRAY-ry
thee-ATA	THEA-ta
she don't	she doesn't (I don't)
she come	she came (I come)
she seen	she saw (I saw)
she done	she did (I did)
sit	Sit down in the chair. Set (lay) the book down.
Leave me go.	Let me go.
belly	STUM-ock
PO-lice	pu-LEECE

Figure 4.2   NCO Spouse Word Choice and Pronunciation Guide
Source: Gross 1980:60.

have active role expectations while junior enlisted wives have passive role expectations.

The historic section of this chapter illustrated the extent to which the original roles for and perceptions of Army spouses depended on social class distinctions. Enlisted soldiers and their spouses likely originated in the lower social classes. Officers' wives tended to come from upper-class families, and their behavior within the military likely replicated that of their family and civilian friends. In addition, their social status was necessary to the upper-class identity of the officer corps. The roles for, and perceptions of, Army spouses suggest that class association still flavors the perceptions and experiences of those spouses on either end of the military rank structure: officers' spouses and enlisted spouses.

Social distinctions in the military parallel civilian social class distinctions. The culturally gendered role expectations vary based on position in this class-like schema. The next important question to ask is whether the class distinctions are creating the role expectations. In the case of junior enlisted spouses, this seems likely. The negative class-based stereotypes are not supportive of an active role in the military community. Further, volunteerism has not been a prominent factor among civilian lower-class and working-class communities. These groups generally focus on taking care of themselves and those close to them (extended family, church members, etc.) and lack the luxury of committing time and resources to assist those that they do not personally know.

The role expectations for officers' spouses have evolved since the time when most officers' wives originated from upper-class families. Some of the traditional roles, such as institutional activities (e.g., volunteering for the Red Cross) and participating in the Officers' Spouse Club, are no longer perceived to be mandatory for most spouses. However, some traditional activities, such as entertaining and socializing, have persisted, and some new activities related to military readiness have been created. The extent to which officers' wives feel compelled to satisfy role expectations differs by the rank and job of the officer: Commanders' wives are most likely to experience significant role expectations and feel compelled to satisfy them.

Do the role expectations of officers' wives' result from class identity? In the past they did, and some still do. To the extent that officers' wives are still expected to entertain and socialize significantly or to participate in the more traditional activities, such as morale, public relations and ceremonial duties, as well as mentoring, development, and role preservation activities, then this is class-related. Such forced participation reflects a need for the image-maintenance of officers as a group and for the cultural maintenance of the very Army system that makes these class-based distinctions. However, the new and extremely time-consuming responsibilities for commanders' wives dealing with the FSG are not class-based. In fact, such activities differ from the volunteerism of civilian upper-class women in that these responsibilities require considerable familiarity and interaction with the enlisted spouses and their families. Civilian upper-class volunteerism tends to assist the less fortunate from a distance, but does not generally involve hands-on assistance to, or interaction with, the lower class (see for example, Ostrander 1984).

French Menu Item	Pronounced	Meaning
FILET	phil-lay	meat without bones
A LA CARTE	ah lah cart	to order dish by dish instead of a preselected complete meal
A LA KING	ah lah king	adding a thick white sauce with peppers, pimentos (sic), mushrooms, and peas
A LA NEWBURG	ah lah newburg	butter and wine
AU GRATIN	oh-grah-ten	usually a baked dish with bread crumbs and cheese sprinkled on top
CANAPE	cana-pay	a small piece of bread or cracker spread with a mixture and eaten as an appetizer
AU JUS	oh-zhu	with its natural juice—usually meat
PATE de FOIE GRAS	pah-tay (it's easier)	liver paste—usually goose liver
HORS D'OEUVRE	or-durv	bite size appetizers
LYONNAISE	lion-aze	finely chopped or sliced onions added
MAITRE D'HOTEL	usually spoken of as the meh-truh dee	the head of the restaurant
MOUSSE	moose	frozen or jellied dish containing well beaten egg whites or whipped cream
PARFAIT	parfay	ice cream with fruit and whipped cream
PETITS FOURS	petty fours	small cakes with icing
SERVICE COMPRIS	ser-vees kohn-pree	the tip is included in the bill

Figure 4.1   NCO Spouse French Menu Glossary
Source: Gross 1980:61–62.

Upper-class women contribute their time to organizing and fund-raising activities, such as boards of directors, and they entertain and socialize for good causes. They do not tend to meet, interact with, or directly associate with those whom they are helping. This is very different from the FSG activities, which compel interaction between officers' spouses and enlisted spouses that was not evident in the Army decades ago. In fact, many wives of retired officers reported to me that they rarely met the wives of enlisted soldiers; sometimes they did not even meet the wives of the more senior enlisted soldiers. Because of the very different nature of FSG activities compared both to the prior role expectations for officers' wives and to the activities of upper-class civilian women, I argue that the FSG responsibilities are not class-based. Instead, they reflect the Army's dire need to respond to their changing situation of increasing numbers of enlisted families and increasing deployment and time away from home in a constrained economic environment. Officers' spouses serve as large-scale uncompensated labor to solve the Army's problems.

Where will the system go from here? Whereas officers' spouses used to fulfill a role that was primarily based on identity justification and appearance, they are now a more integral part of the Army mechanism. They have become uncompensated, compulsory labor to an extent unseen previously. This use/abuse of officers' spouses is a response to the needs of the rest of the Army community families, but it is necessitated by the relatively pure military need to support mission readiness. Thus, in the course of responding to the increasing demographic diversity in the military community, the Army culture is no longer as class-based. While this might initially be applauded as conforming to general U.S. society, which prefers to obscure or deny class identity, the Army is actually an anomaly moving away from popular society. By compelling officers' wives to participate in uncompensated labor, the Army is diverging from a society that supports and increasingly compensates professional working women.

Notes

1. The methodology for this work is described in greater detail in Harrell (2000a and 2000b). In sum, this work is the result of transcribed interviews with over one hundred spouses and additional interviews with hundreds of military personnel, DoD employees, and others around the military community. The research was conducted primarily at Fort Drum, New York, and at Fort Stewart, Georgia. This chapter resulted from dissertation research completed at the University of Virginia in 2000. Thus, this research was not a RAND study, but was funded in part by

the National Science Foundation and the Center for Children, Families, and the Law, University of Virginia. The opinions expressed are solely the author's and do not represent RAND or any of its sponsors.

2. For brevity, this work focuses on officer and junior enlisted spouses, omitting senior enlisted, or noncommissioned, spouses who occupy an in-between status.

3. One historical accounting found that less than 31 percent of the entering classes at West Point during the period 1842 to 1887 had fathers who were bankers, manufacturers, judges, merchants, congressmen, lawyers, or diplomats. This compares to more than half of Annapolis fathers of the same time period representing these highly esteemed professions (Coffman 1986:222).

4. Hence the discomfort at unexpected (and thus unreciprocated) Christmas gifts or gifts of markedly unequal value.

5. Senior personnel can make it difficult for junior enlisted personnel to marry, however. One recently retired Navy officer explained that when young sailors meet a girl abroad that they want to marry, noncommissioned officers and commanders will often keep that sailor aboard ship until either he changes his mind or the ship leaves port.

6. This benefit was taken away after World War II, and reinstated in 1950 at the advent of the Korean War (Alt and Stone: 98, 104, 111).

7. Janowitz's discussion of this segregation is especially interesting because it says more about the attitudes of the 1950s and 1960s, during which he wrote, than about the time of the segregation. His logic for why segregation was bad is not that the children of enlisted families are just like officers' children and thus deserve equal education, but that the "son of every family is potentially an officer" (Janowitz 1971 [1960]:180). In other words, they don't necessarily deserve to be included, but some day they might be one of us, so we should not exclude them now.

8. The discussion of officer spouse roles is largely excerpted from Harrell (2001), where these activities are described in more detail.

9. The battalion and brigade commanders and spouses interviewed who budgeted or kept track of social expenses typically mentioned $300 to $400 per month.

10. Family Support Groups have recently been redesignated as Family Readiness Groups, but this work maintains the original designation to be consistent with the original materials and to the interview transcripts.

11. It is worth noting that having an upper-class identity does not necessarily imply financial resources or compensation commensurate with much of the civilian upper class.

12. Noncommissioned officers, or NCOs, are senior enlisted soldiers.

13. The Army fraternization policy prohibits relationships to include socializing between soldiers of different ranks if perceived to compromise supervisory authority or potentially result in preferential treatment.

14. This handbook is over twenty years old and thus some of the social attitudes have likely changed. Nonetheless, the material is still illuminating for the perceptions of NCO wives and junior enlisted wives that it portrays.

References Cited

Alt, Betty Sowers, and Bonnie Domrose Stone. 1991. *Campfollowing: A History of the Military Wife*. New York: Praeger.

Bourg, Mary C. 1995. "Male Tokens in a Masculine Environment: Men with Military Mates." Paper presented at the 1995 annual meeting of the American Sociological Association.

Clark, Maurine. 1956. *Captain's Bride, General's Lady*. New York: McGraw-Hill.

Cline, Lydia Sloan. 1995. *Today's Military Wife: Meeting the Challenges of Service Life*. Mechanicsburg, PA: Stackpole Books.

Coffman, Edward M. 1986. *The Old Army: A Portrait of the American Army in Peacetime, 1784–1898*. New York: Oxford University Press.

Collins, Randall. 1992. "Women and the Production of Status Cultures." In *Cultivating Differences: Symbolic Boundaries and the Making of Inequality*. Michele Lamont and Marcel Fournier, eds. Pp. 213–231. Chicago: The University of Chicago Press.

Combs, Ann. 1981. *Smith College Never Taught Me How to Salute*. New York: Harper & Row.

Crossley, Ann and Carol A. Keller. 1993. *The Army Wife Handbook: A Complete Social Guide*. 2nd ed. Sarasota, Florida: ABI Press.

Durand, Doris Briley. 1995. "The Role of the Army Wife as Perceived by Male Officers and Their Wives: Is it a Commitment to the 'Two-For-One' Career Pattern?" Ph.D. dissertation. Department of Sociology, University of Maryland, College Park, Maryland.

Evans-Pritchard, E. E. 1970. "Sexual Inversion Among the Azande," in *American Anthropologist*, 72:1428–1434.

———. 1971. *The Azande: History and Political Institutions*. Oxford: Clarendon Press.

Garrett, Pamela C. 1986. "Unissued Baggage." *Marine Corps Gazette*. February: 56–60.

Gibbons, Sheila. 1984. "Commanders' Wives." *Ladycom*. June:51–58, 63–65, 70.

Gross, Mary Preston. 1980. *Mrs. NCO*. Chulota, FL: Beau Lac Publishers.

Harrell, Margaret C. 2001. "Army Officers' Spouses: Have the White Gloves Been Mothballed?" *Armed Forces & Society*, 28:1.

Harrell, Margaret C. 2000a. "Brass Rank and Gold Rings: Class, Race, Gender and Kinship Within the Army Community." Ph.D. dissertation, University of Virginia, Charlottesville.

———. 2000b. *Invisible Women: Junior Enlisted Army Wives*. Santa Monica, CA: RAND.

Janowitz, Morris. 1971 [1960]. *The Professional Soldier: A Social and Political Portrait*. New York: Free Press.

Kinzer, Betty, and Marion Leach. 1966. *What Every Army Wife Should Know*. Harrisburg, PA: Stackpole Books.

Kirby, Sheila Nataraj, and Harry J. Thie. 1996. *Enlisted Personnel Management: A Historical Perspective*. Santa Monica, CA: RAND.

Lane, Lydia Spencer. 1987. *I Married a Soldier*. Albuquerque, NM: The University of New Mexico Press.

Little, Roger W. 1971. "The Military Family." In. *Handbook of Military Institutions*. R. W. Little, ed. Pp. Beverly Hills, California: SAGE Publications.

Marshall, Katherine Tupper. 1946. *Together: Annals of an Army Wife*. New York: Tupper and Love, Inc.

Mauss, Marcel. 1990 [1950]. *The Gift*. W. D. Halls, trans. New York: W.W. Norton.

Murray, Stephen O. and Will Roscoe (eds.). 1998. *Boy-Wives and Female Husbands: Studies of African Homosexualities*. New York: St. Martin's Press.

Murphy, Mary Kay, and Carol Bowles Parker. 1966. *Fitting In as a New Service Wife*. Harrisburg, PA: Stackpole Books.

Ortner, Sherry B. 1991. "Reading America: Preliminary Notes on Class and Culture." In *Recapturing Anthropology*. Richard G. Fox, ed. Pp. 163–189. Sante Fe, NM: School of American Research.

Ostrander, Susan A. 1984. *Women of the Upper Class*. Philadelphia: Temple University Press.

Riley, R. 1988. "Military Wives in Revolt: Service Spouses Want to Do More than Pour Afternoon Tea." *U.S. News & World Report*. April 18:38.

Rosenberg, Florence R. 1989. *The Wife of the First Term Enlisted Soldier: A Study of Socialization and Role*. Washington, DC: Department of Military Psychiatry, Walter Reed Army Institute of Research.

Shea, Nancy. 1954. *The Army Wife*. New York: Harper & Brothers.

———. 1966. *The Army Wife*. New York: Harper & Brothers.

Summerhayes, Martha. 1911. *Vanished Arizona: Recollections of My Army Life*. Salem, MA: The Salem Press Co.

United States Army. 1993a. *A Guide to Establishing Family Support Groups*. DA-PAM 608–47.

———. 1993b. *The Army Family Readiness Handbook*. College Station, TX: Texas A&M University.

Weinstein, Laurie, and Helen Mederer. 1997. "Blue Navy Blues: Submarine Officers and the Two-Person Career." In *Wives and Warriors: Women and the Military in the United States and Canada*. L. Weinstein and C. C. White, eds. Pp. 7–18. Westport, CT: Bergin & Garvey.

CHAPTER 5

Weight Control and Physical Readiness Among Navy Personnel

Joshua Linford-Steinfeld

Tell me what you eat and I'll tell you what you are.
—A quote by the famous gastronomic philosopher
Brillat-Savarin (1755–1826), reprinted on an
opening page of the sourcebook for a discontinued
Navy Weight Management Program

An Ethnographic Entrance

In the parking lot of a Naval Medical Center (NMCSD), which is located on top of a hill in Balboa Park in San Diego, California, there is a sign that reads "Wellness Aerobics, walk and burn 08 calories from here to N.H.S.D. Main Courtyard." From one perspective, such a sign might seem absurd. After all, eight calories is about the equivalent of licking an envelope to seal it. From another perspective, if every person utilizing NMCSD, which includes active-duty Navy and Marine personnel, dependents, and retirees, were to park a little farther away, take the stairs, and make other minor adjustments to their lifestyles, the calorie burn over time might be significant enough to help with weight control. Whichever perspective you choose, the sign is part of the institutionalization of a trajectory toward a certain kind of definition of health. The sign reflects a larger debate taking place in the armed forces surrounding how to keep active duty personnel physically ready for their daily jobs and for potential deployment: What kind of physical readiness and weight control standards and requirements need to be in place, and how should they be enforced?

In this chapter I investigate the relationship of weight control, physical readiness, and bodily practice to: discipline and regimentation (eating and exercise practices); "disordered" eating; and gender, among men in the United States Navy. Along with individuals, I examine policy, the health care system, and daily institutional operations (e.g., remedial fitness programs). As I have recently finished fieldwork, this chapter is a preliminary critical essay on which I will build future work. I combine the description of an approach that can be used to think through anthropology of the military that focuses on the body with pertinent background research. I buttress the description and research with analysis of ethnographic examples. As such, I aim to provide an overview that raises and situates salient questions and serves as an opening rather than as an endpoint.

While there has been quantitative research and some limited qualitative research on weight control and physical readiness in the armed forces, there has been virtually no ethnographically based anthropological study of these topics in the United States (Marriott 1994, 1995). My research involves extensive fieldwork on naval bases as well as onboard vessels and includes both participant-observation and in-depth qualitative interviews. It aims to discover what sort of relation the discourses and diagnoses surrounding eating, weight, masculinity, and disorder—as they are expressed in military policy, psychiatry, and popular culture—bear to the actual lived experience of men and how this relation intersects with the social construction of the body. Moving beyond the categories of "overweight" and "underweight," I take eating and exercise to include an entire range of practices, rituals, and affective states related to weight gain and loss, muscularity and body-building, and the ingestion of other substances (i.e., tobacco, caffeine). Grounded fieldwork in a range of settings allows gender, order, and "disorder" to be read through and against the body and society (i.e., on a continuum), without (re)generating dichotomies (e.g., normal/ pathological, masculine/feminine, gay/straight). Further, ethnography allows order, gender, and their adherent dichotomies to be analyzed beyond the often over-simplifying tendencies of the medical model (i.e., labeling people as sick or healthy or defining addiction just as a disease).

Background

Weight control is a salient issue for Navy personnel. Physical readiness, defined as being within weight standards and passing a physical fitness test, is measured twice yearly and is often used to grant or deny promotions. On surface and subsurface vessels, exercise options are limited by space constraints, and food is both abundant and a form of entertainment. Navy personnel who fail to meet body composition or physical fitness standards or who have "eating disorders" may be denied promotions or may be administratively discharged. They may also impede operational readiness. Although the Navy does have mandatory physical training and voluntary weight management programs for "over-fat" personnel, it does not have structured treatment for eating disorders. Those with eating disorders often seek treatment in civilian mental health clinics.

In the Navy, the prevalence of eating-disordered behavior among enlisted men and women exceeds the prevalence of these behaviors in civilian men and women (respectively), even accounting for eating problems that predated military service (McNulty 1997a,b, 2000). Captain McNulty found clinically diagnosable eating disorders to be extremely prevalent among active-duty Navy men: 2.5 percent for anorexia nervosa and 6.5 percent for bulimia nervosa (McNulty 1997a). Rates for civilian women are 1 to 2 percent and 2 to 3 percent, respectively (with civilian women being 6 to 10 times more likely to develop either anorexia or bulimia as compared to civilian men). Some researchers have asserted that 54 percent of military personnel are overweight (based on medically accepted standards—body mass index) and 6.2 percent are obese, with the Navy having the highest percentages of any armed forces branch (*Los Angeles Times* 2002). There is vast disagreement about the number of overweight and obese personnel. Debates include but are not limited to the scientific validity of definitions of overweight and obesity, the accuracy and precision of measuring body composition, and the disparity between statistics collected by the Navy (some of which are based on self-report and some on data from the body composition testing) and by other researchers. Proportionately, more men than women are overweight in the military, with the reverse being true in civilian society (*Los Angeles Times* 2002). Physical readiness standards potentially foster excessive exercise. McNulty (1997a) states that use of laxatives, diet pills, vomiting, and fasting to meet standards increased during the body measurement periods but remained at disturbingly high rates year-round. The rates of subclinical eating problems in the Navy are impossible to determine. However, the effects of such subclinical problems may be more wide ranging than clinical obesity and diagnosable eating disorders.

Additionally, the Naval Health Research Center (NHRC) has generated a substantial body of primarily quantitative literature on the topics of weight control, physical readiness, and health practices. The studies are presented to illustrate the progression of the field from the early 1980s and to show the relevance of studying men and weight in the Navy. In 1984 Hoiberg, Berard, Watten, and Caine showed that a Navy-sponsored program was relatively successful in aiding weight loss during treatment and throughout a one-year follow-up. In response to the naval instruction that changed the standards from height/weight measurement to a body fat standard, estimated from neck and abdominal circumference, Hogdon and Marcinik (1983) conducted a study that found that the change would not greatly affect the number of personnel on weight control programs. Along with Marcinik, Hogdon and O'Brien (1985) found that while the majority of vessels were well equipped with exercise facilities, they were under utilized due to a lack of command-sponsored conditioning programs for the entire crew. In a 1986 NHRC study, Conway, Dutton, and Briggs gathered information about the sailors' perceptions of the Navy's Health and Physical Readiness Program. Main criticisms of the program included lack of time to exercise and lack of fair enforcement standards and participation across ranks. A 1988 study by Trent and Conway that studied 1,013 shipboard men found that participants tended to skip breakfast, ingested moderate amounts of caffeine, and preferred a low-fiber and high-fat diet. Moreover, diet was a significant predictor of fitness, even after controlling for tobacco use and exercise. A survey of Command Fitness Coordinators by Conway, Trent, and Cronan (1989) revealed that many commands lacked remedial exercise programs and healthful food choices. In 1990, DuBois, Goodman, and Conway collaborated on a study that indicated that overweight males consumed less carbohydrates (preferring fat or protein) than lean males and that overweight subjects were more likely to engage in emotional eating. Further, Dubois and Goodman's (1989) study of 153 individuals showed a strong relationship between being overweight and obesity-prone food behaviors (e.g., food obsessions), family obesity, and low socioeconomic level. In a study of 1,292 male and female active-duty personnel, self-esteem and quality of life were positively associated with exercise (Stevens and Conway 1991). A longitudinal study by Trent and Hurtado (1997) between 1983 and 1994 concluded that the Navy's health promotion efforts have had a significant positive impact on the health and fitness of Navy personnel, although women's health was significantly better than men's for a number of factors. In a sample of 1,292 Navy and Marine Corps men and women, Graham, Hourani, and Yuan (1999) determined that Navy women tended to meet weight standards more often than Navy men. Brosch (1998) has examined physical activity in active duty female soldiers.

The studies just discussed suggest that weight control and physical readiness, particularly among active-duty men, is an arena that could benefit from qualitative research. These studies were primarily statistical; my work builds on previous research, particularly that of McNulty, by examining eating and exercise within the context of everyday behaviors, without presupposing a distinct boundary between normal and disordered behavior. Anthropological research should not be viewed as oppositional to these quantitative studies, but rather as a complementary modality.

Males and Eating Disorders

Over the past twenty-five years, there has been a great deal of attention in both the scientific community and in popular society on the two officially diagnosable "eating disorders," anorexia and bulimia, and more recently on binge-eating disorder (BED has been suggested for inclusion in the Diagnostic and Statistic Manual of Mental Disorders (DSM), the standard diagnostic reference manual used by mental health providers). The commonly held notion that eating disorders affect women almost exclusively is reflected in both the mass media and the lack of scientific literature pertaining to men with eating disorders. Just as it is critical not to exclude an entire series of bodily practices when discussing disordered eating, it is also necessary to situate men, male sexuality, and masculinity within a domain that has been construed in relation to "women" and the "feminine." Men are part of the history of hysteria, hypochondria, and disordered eating. Some pertinent examples: One of the patients with nervous consumption Morton (1689/1694) describes was male, as was a patient of Robert Whytt, some seventy-five years later (Silverman 1990); Showalter's examination of "male hysterics" (1997); the quasi-fictional exploration of post–World War I "shell-shock" in male soldiers by Pat Barker (1991); and recent accounts of male body image issues, such as *Making Weight: Men's Conflicts with Food, Weight, Shape, and Appearance* (Andersen, Cohn, and Holbrook 2000) and *The Adonis Complex: The Secret Crisis of Male Body Obsession* (Pope, Phillips, and Olivardia 2000).

Whether there is a "secret crisis" that needs to be exposed remains to be seen. However, it is worth examining how a renewed emphasis on the male body may or may not be part of a broader societal shift, especially within a media-driven environment, hyper-focused on size, image, and "health."

Statistics, however, indicate that one in ten individuals affected by the officially recognized eating disorders are men, a ratio that rises to one in two for binge-eating disorder (Andersen 1999). As with much statistical information, it is difficult to know how well data on eating disorders represent what is actually occurring on the ground. In the case of men, the statistics may be biased by multiple factors. As there is a lack of scientific literature on men with eating disorders, healthcare providers may not be diagnosing men, especially because much of the general literature identifies disordered eating as a woman's or a "gay" man's problem. The criteria and tools for diagnosing eating disorders may be gender biased. For instance, the criteria suggest that not menstruating is a useful diagnostic symptom. This is certainly not useful for diagnosing men, and may not even be especially useful in diagnosing women if a schema of behaviors and attitudes is present without menstrual cessation. Eating disorders may be under-reported by people affected because these behaviors are marked by secrecy. Moreover, the boundaries of what constitutes a pathological problem versus normal dieting and weight-control are obscure. Additionally, practices related to physical fitness, which are usually viewed as constructive, may in fact be part of a destructive trajectory, as in the cases of compulsive exercise or "reverse anorexia," characterized by an obsessive focus on muscle size and definition.

Diagnostic criteria seem to assume that "eating disorders" are an objective set of facts that exist exterior to the language of diagnosis. While the language of diagnosis does offer a common way to communicate, criteria are a systematically manufactured construction in which symptoms are perceived as a cohesive functional entity rather than as a delineated method of classification. As such, my focus on the "diagnosable" eating disorders is not intended to be exclusionary of other more or less "ordered" practices associated with weight, muscularity, or the body—obesity, binge eating, bodybuilding, surgery, and the like. While it is important not to disavow the accounts and experiences of people's bodily practices in a given place in a given time, it is necessary to challenge the ways psychological and biomedical explanations of such experiences claim to purvey a notion of "absolute truth." The inclusions and exclusions surrounding disordered eating and the construction of gender demand further investigation from a perspective that does not privilege a psychological or diagnostic framing of either history or people inside (or outside, if that is possible) institutional settings. There has been virtually no ethnographically based anthropological study of men with eating disorders in the United States. The military environment makes more complex the issues surrounding eating, weight, and gender. Historically, both sociology and psychology have relied on the military as a source from which to obtain participants for both military and nonmilitary related studies. The military along with the importance of physical readiness is a unique arena for anthropological research.

Methods

I accessed staff and line communities at three primary sites: the Naval Medical Center San Diego (NMCSD), the largest Naval medical facility on the West Coast (primarily staff); Naval Station San Diego, at 32nd Street (NAVSTA), the primary West Coast facility for surface vessels; and Naval Submarine Base, Point Loma (PL)—San Diego, the primary facility for submarines. I spent approximately nine months at NMCSD and two months at NAVSTA and PL, respectively. The major part of each day at least four days of each week was spent at a site. Subjects of all rates and ranks, excluding minors and new recruits who had not completed basic training, were interviewed and/or accompanied during their daily activities. Military-affiliated civil service staff and contractors (male and female) were also interviewed and shadowed to establish ethnographic context. Subsites at NMCSD, included the dining facility (mess hall), the Nutrition Management Department, the offices associated with health promotion (e.g., sitting in on nutrition classes, investigating the production of written health-related materials), the physical readiness testing units, other eating establishments at NMCSD (McDonald's, Subway, etc.), and exercise facilities (including men's locker rooms and indoor and outdoor exercise areas).

Data came primarily from documented observations. I took field notes that described settings and specific behaviors and documented conversations. A second set of notes included more reflexive, subjective thoughts and observations. To avoid disruption, I did not take field notes during interactions except to serve as reminders of the sequence of events. I wrote detailed field notes following encounters or at the end of the day. For instance, in the physical readiness testing units, I made observations surrounding the design and implementation of testing procedures, including body composition and physical readiness testing. I observed both personnel conducting the procedures, as well as those being tested. I also observed the Fitness Enhancement Program classes (aerobic exercise) via participation, along with mock physical fitness testing.

I conducted extensive interviews with willing active-duty shore and sea personnel and with other Department of Defense personnel. These interviews did not follow a formal questionnaire format but were highly flexible to accommodate the interests and speech patterns of each subject. The fundamental goal of these interviews was to explore how people understand and articulate their experiences and positions in the military and in the broader context of society. Interviews were audiotaped with the permission of subjects. Interactions ranged from one to many encounters throughout the time frame of the research, and interviews lasted from thirty minutes to two hours or more.

Ethnographic Examples

Some Not-So-Thin Descriptions of a Naval Hospital

The complexity of issues surrounding physical readiness and weight control becomes apparent as I burn off my eight calories and enter the NMCSD (NHSD) courtyard. As I walk through the parking lot, I notice the glass-enclosed building designated for smokers. The courtyard itself is pristine and there is a great deal of activity: There are active duty and civilian staff person-nel returning from running in Balboa Park; healthcare providers, patients, and staff move from place to place, sit on stone benches, and purchase food. There are a few kiosks—a flower stand, a cart that sells small gifts, and an automatic teller machine (ATM). A Seattle's Best Coffee Stand and a Krispy Kreme Donut cart are being installed next to the ATM. To the right of your caffeine fix, there is a building that houses a TCBY Yogurt and a Subway (there are run-of-the-mill doughnuts available here as well). The Subway windows dis-play three advertisement posters: The center one shows a large pastrami sub and indicates that it comes with half a pound of meat; the poster to the right informs me that Subway is a proud sponsor of the American Heart Association Walk; and the poster to the left says "Stay Fit, Stay Fresh."

Back toward the main entrance to the courtyard, a sign directs people down a flight of stairs to a neon-light–decorated McDonald's. The McDonald's exits into an interior hallway, and a few yards down is a NEX store—the equivalent of a convenience store—replete with an entire aisle of candy, which sit conveniently next to the "healthy" energy bars. One of the dietitians I interviewed stated that this NEX is one of the largest candy sellers of any NEX in the world. Back on the main level, directly above the McDonald's is the mess hall. As you enter the mess hall, a large neon sign reads "Welcome to the Navy's Finest Medical Dining Facility"; a smaller neon sign hangs from the ceiling reading "Desserts." The glass dessert cabinet includes slices of pie as well as dishes of cottage cheese garnished with fruit. On the wall to the left is a sign explaining how fat levels are coded. Each menu item is coded as green, yellow, or red, which corresponds to low, medium, and high fat content. The mess hall has both a regular entrée line and a separate fast-food line. There is a salad bar and a limited selection of fresh fruit.

Outside of the main courtyard, another eight to twelve calories away, is Building 26, the basement of which houses the gym. Gymgoers pass by several vending machines to enter the space. There are no diet choices in the soda machine. Another NEX that stocks a wide selection of bodybuilding products (powders, supplements, and the like), a Pizza Hut, and a Rice King (Chinese fast food) also occupy the building. NMCSD is not unique among bases in San Diego; most have fast food and some have GNC stores (General Nutrition Centers) that sell an even wider variety of "health" products than the NEX, including products with stimulants, the safety of which is widely debated.

On one hand, the convenience and choice available at NMCSD allows the campus to be self-contained on top of this hill, provides a source of entertainment, and meets the desires and requests of military staff (which influences morale), all at fairly reasonable prices. The mess hall is by far the best value, with prices essentially set to the cost of the food plus a small fee for disposal costs. On the other hand, a military family of four can consume an enormous number of calories and fat grams at one of the fast food establishments, which, while efficient and cheap, does little for fostering healthy eating habits. Hospitals can be very stressful places, whether you are staff, patient, or visitor, and when faced with paradoxical and mixed messages, choosing that six-inch turkey sub with no mayo rather than the pastrami, followed by a couple of Krispy Kreme doughnuts or a bag of candy, poses a serious challenge. Additional emotional factors around food and body image add to a dizzying set of issues surrounding autonomy, choice, control, and worthiness. The blending of the civilian and military arenas generates choices that have broad-ranging effects. This is not a "you-eat-what-gets-put-on-your-tray" military environment.

The environment both challenges the need and the desire of the Navy to create and maintain an ordered individual (the lean, mean, fighting machines who look "sharp" in their uniforms) and helps maintain a sense of order among individuals and within the institution (e.g., keeps morale high) by offering "the men" what they want without disrupting efficiency (fast-food)—but at what other costs? How can weight control and physical readiness standards, which inherently require discipline and regimentation, be adhered to in such a paradoxical environment? How might such paradoxes contribute to eating problems with effects ranging from obesity to anorexia and bulimia? I do not mean to imply that this environment is the only reason for the development of eating issues among Navy personnel. Such an assertion would be analogous to saying that media images, such as fashion ads, are solely responsible for eating disorders among teenage women.

Managing Weight

There have been several evolutions of the weight management program in the Navy. While there is not space here to elucidate a full history, it is important to note that "compulsive overeating" used to be treated along with alcohol and drug problems at the Substance Abuse Rehabilitation Department at Point Loma. "Compulsive overeating" is not an official diagnosis, so personnel were admitted to treatment under the diagnosis of obesity (interview, January 14, 2002). According to various interviews, the program moved from a six-week day-treatment program, to a four-week program, to a two-week intensive outpatient program (meeting every day). The program is now under the auspices of the Health Promotion Department at NMCSD. The current program is known as Track III, a ten- to thirteen-week completely outpatient program in which the participants meet once a week for a few hours. There are also two less intensive, or lower, levels of the weight management program. Track II involves one-on-one sessions with a nutritionist and/or exercise physiologist, and Track I is an educational program focused on basic nutritional principles. Track I at NMCSD is attended primarily by retirees and other Department of Defense beneficiaries, such as military wives who want to slim down before their husbands come home from sea duty. The reasons for the program changes—both the reduction in intensity and the switch from "treatment" to "education" are complex and include both monetary issues and optimization—a desire of commands to limit the amount of time personnel were taken away from work duties. The efficacy and long-term outcomes of the more intensive programs were also questioned, and overweight personnel resisted being grouped with alcoholics and labeled as addicts. The general attitude that was often conveyed to active-duty personnel, according to my interviews with war-fighters as well as both civilian and active duty support staff, was that weight is a personal problem, and it is the responsibility of the individual to "take care of the problem." The intensity level of treatment programs has steadily decreased; obesity in the Navy remains high.

The Navy does offer a remedial fitness program for personnel who can not seem to "take care of it" on their own. At NMCSD, the program consists of hour-and-a-half-long exercise sessions three times a week and is command directed (mandatory) if one fails the body composition or physical readiness test. Adherence to the command order is sporadic at best, resulting in generally low attendance, except for the weeks prior to the next testing cycle. According to the trainers (Command Fitness Leaders, [CFLs]), this sudden increase of exercisers, who often have been relatively sedentary since the last testing cycle, results in an increase of orthopedic injuries.

Program attendance seems dependent on numerous factors. For instance, if the commanding officer considers physical fitness a priority, then adherence is good. However, if a department is short-staffed or if the person responsible for getting personnel of that department to attend the exercise sessions is also out of standards, then adherence may be poor. The CFLs often fail in their attempts to promote adherence to the program. Directing higher-ranking personnel to exercise goes against the hierarchical grain, and CFLs are labeled as "fitness Nazis" if they push too hard in their attempts to foster participation or in the intensity of the actual exercise regime. Many trainers expressed their frustration and felt they were fighting an uphill battle that was impossible to win.

Shipshape

On the ships, the supply officers are able to provide a wide variety of choices, but often need to use up fresh foods first before they spoil and then rely on frozen foods (often fried) until resupply is available. While some personnel may have both time and the incentive to exercise, food is one of the few rewards of ship life. As one health promotions staff member told me, when one ship tried to remove sliders (hamburgers) from the menu, the ship went "crazy." Maintaining what this staff member identified as "customer satisfaction" becomes a way to maintain order. Recipes are often not prepared according to the Department of Defense regulations (orders), but rather based on the "suggestions" of personnel, including both the eaters of the food and the mess cooks themselves. Taking and giving orders becomes infused with new meanings—it allows for regulating order by not adhering to regulations. "Higher-ups" keep their "customers" satisfied (maintain order among the ranks by keeping them from going "crazy") through a kind of taking of orders (or at least allowing some slack). At the same time, all personnel are given orders to adhere to specific weight and physical readiness standards. So, while food consumption is one of few ways personnel can direct themselves (e.g., placing their own orders), they are simultaneously being given directions (e.g., orders) about what to weigh and how fit to be. There is a kind of trading—you can have the foods you desire, a sense of being able to order your own body through some sense of personal control and choice in a highly controlled environment, but you are responsible for not letting your weight get out of control. However, there is often little time to work out, and personnel "wolf down" a slider or two in between filling orders. Life on submarines poses further challenges; food is one of the few sources of entertainment and is plentiful, and there is little or no space to exercise. One fast-attack sub I visited had a single exercise bike crammed into a corner. While some men exercised—one man told me he did several hundred push-ups a day—time constraints and fatigue make eating and sleeping priorities. Back on shore, surface and subsurface personnel can head for the nearest base to get the "real" fast food they have not had access to at sea. While some men hit the gym once back home, time with families and keeping their civilian lives in order often takes precedence. Eating and exercise become mechanisms through which choice, will, and order are expressed.

Implications and Applications

The preceding descriptions and interpretations illustrate how the seemingly everydayness of things is part of an array of intricate and layered factors that have broad-ranging implications. An anthropological approach produces knowledge about weight, disorder, and gender as they relate to the consuming body/subject in late capitalist society. Such knowledge can contribute to furthering research in the social and military sciences by demonstrating an approach that stakes legitimate claims without generating analysis that is too closed or too open. Potentially, such knowledge and analysis will influence policy for healthcare, health promotion, and allowable reasons for discharge for operational forces in the Navy and other military services.

Anthropology?

My research relates to the work of other anthropologists in two subfields of anthropology: medical anthropology and psychological anthropology. What my work adds to these well-established subfields is a topic and an approach that generates links between and among these subfields. I interpret "anthropology" broadly and include figures who fall outside of the disciplinary boundary of "traditional" anthropology, but who are clearly influential within the discipline. In terms of anthropology of the body, my research involves the problem of how to integrate physicality into an analysis of "culture." For instance, in Marcel Mauss's seminal essay (1973 [1934]) on techniques of the body, he argues that the body has no natural form; rather, the body is a self-fashioning instrument. What constitutes disordered eating among Navy men is a question directly related to Mauss's assertions pertaining to naturalness and the way in which the bodies are (self-)created. More recently, Csordas (1990) has proposed embodiment as a way to analyze the dualistic relationship between the body and culture, and Scheper-Hughes and Lock (1987) have postulated that the individual, social, and political body must be acknowledged in investigating formations of suffering. Whether military or civilian, men with eating problems inhabit bodies that are simultaneously theirs and not theirs, bodies that bear inscriptions of culture (and suffering) that simultaneously produce culture. War and all of its preparations may etch these inscriptions deeper. Eating disorders can be considered part of a constellation of bio-cultural events that are integrally linked to personality and the psyche of subjects. (See Kleinman's [1988] description of a model for integrating experience and biocultural events.) However, individual subjects and culture are mutually constitutive entities, meaning subjects and culture simultaneously influence and change one another. As such, both subjects and culture are constantly in flux. Many bio-cultural events are intertwined with sex and gender, the study of which is reflective of the importance of the relationship between subjectivity and the body. My work adds to anthropology by generating a collage that can describe and interpret the relationships among the body, the subject, and culture without dissolving the tensions among them.

For instance, discipline and regimentation are intimately related to the body and subjectivity. Regimentation can be used to control behaviors (e.g., three meals a day), but extreme regimentation in terms of exercise and food consumption may lead to "abnormal" behaviors. Discipline and regimentation relate to the construction of order (e.g., taking orders, ordering through regimentation, maintaining order, placing food orders) and disorder (i.e., how might discipline and regimentation both contribute to eating disorders and at the same time be deployed as strategies to treat them?). A further issue at stake concerns the roles of masculinity, gender, and sexuality in the construction of the body (e.g., muscularity) and the subject through exercise and other disciplinary practices. What is the relationship of gender (and masculinity) to disordered eating in the Navy, for individuals and for the institution? Psychiatry links the development of eating disorders in men to sexual identity and sexuality conflicts. Both "coming out" as gay and admitting to an eating disorder can result in discharge from the Navy. Moreover, as discussed in the background section, there is a high prevalence of eating disorders among Navy men (equal or greater to that of civilian women, depending on the specific diagnosis and how statistics are calculated). But the threat of discharge results in a rhetoric of secrecy analogous to the "don't ask, don't tell" policy.

Discipline and regimentation are part of a constellation of questions that can be addressed through anthropological study of the Navy. Some of the possible specific questions where anthropology can be utilized include: (1) What practices and habits related to eating and exercise, including use of substances (e.g., tobacco, diuretics), do male active-duty Navy personnel utilize for weight control? (2) Specifically, what perceptions and attitudes do active-duty Navy males have regarding weight control practices, physical readiness standards, and their bodies? (3) On a broader level, what is the relationship between the body and the culture of the Navy? (4) What are the similarities and differences between war fighters (unrestricted line) and support personnel in terms of weight control and physical readiness?, and (5) Within the war fighting community, what are the similarities and differences between surface and sub-surface active duty men?

Theory

I assert that there is a triangular relationship among the individual physical body, the collective "body" of the Navy, and the larger social body, with complex relations existing among these distinct bodies (See figure 5.1). Within this triangular framework, I assert that subjects both form and are formed by the complex interactions of internal psychic drives, existential experience, and external forces and structures. My perspective acknowledges the fundamental roles of loss and excess, paradox and conflict, and normativity and error as they pertain to eating behaviors. In relation to ingestion, exercise, and bodily practices, I approach the body, subjectivity (i.e., the self), and society as conjunctures of risk and potential (e.g., loss and gain, etc.). I seek to understand the interplay of discourses and domains of lived experience within these conjunctures by describing and interpreting them. This approach entails an attention to bodily, institutional, disciplinary, and discursive practices surrounding consumption in everyday life and within specific institutions; historical and current popular culture representations of the body, both visual and written; and gender and psychiatric theory in relation to deviance, normalcy, and normativity. I do not juxtapose gay and straight or masculine and feminine. Rather, I attempt to crosscut each of these dichotomies by examining configurations of sexualities in relation to the

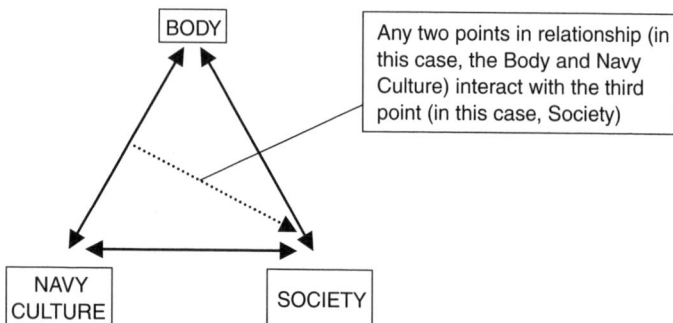

Figure 5.1 Triangular Relationship of the "Body"

body, the military, and broader society. I question dichotomies and frame bodily practices in terms of degrees, kinds, tones, and variances. In order to avoid re-creating such dichotomies in my analysis, I work from a nonreductive theoretical perspective that allows for complexity without rendering opaque conclusions that fail to address what happens on the ground. I draw from a number of views of subjectivity, without giving primacy to any one of them: the idea that subjectivity is experiential or existential, as in the psychoanalytic formulations of Freud (1960 [1901]) or the phenomenological formulations regarding embodiment, such as those proposed by Ludwig Binswanger (1958 [1944]) or Thomas Csordas (1990); that subjectivity is partially based on cognition and behavior; that it is formulated primarily by discourses through the Foucaldian notions of subjectivation and biopolitics (Foucault 1978); that the body is the essential site of subjectivity; Susan Bordo's feminist rendering of the construction of female and male bodies (1993, 1999); George Canguilhem's (1989) notions of error and norm in relation to the construction of the subject; and Jacques Lacan's (1977 [1966]) and Michel de Certeau's (1984) reformulations of Freudian psychoanalysis (particularly in terms of loss and pleasure).

Situated at the intersection of subjective experience and the discursive and material fields (which constitute, enable, and limit such experience), my work charts the complex interaction of gender, consumption, diagnosis, and techniques of the self (e.g., discipline). My ethnographic research investigates a critical and uncharted domain—the connections between American psychiatric and military arenas, as they relate to gender and disordered eating. Through a historically grounded account of how men construct and are constructed by behaviors and values (e.g., eating, sex, aggression, will, loss, order), it addresses the way in which lived experience is mediated by pervasive discourses surrounding eating disorders (e.g., diagnostic categories, treatment paradigms), weight, and gender.

Policy

This work also has the potential to inform policy changes. What follows is a sampling of interrelated (and often conflicting) issues and perspectives that indicate areas for possible policy evaluation or reevaluation. There is general consensus that physical readiness is important for the Navy, although some believe that body composition and physical readiness testing standards should be more job-specific and better adjusted for age and gender. There is concern about differentials between how weight control issues are handled among enlisted personnel compared with officers. For instance, there is a perception that officers receive special treatment (e.g., are not held to the same weight control standards) because they are of higher rank, are more indispensable because of their job duties, or can utilize intimidation to get more "wiggle room" during testing. Many personnel see standardization as a potential way to alleviate unfair treatment (e.g., have testing and measurement done by an outside contractor rather than Navy personnel). Yet personnel of varying rates and ranks often believe that their individual circumstances warrant special consideration. There is concern, especially among Navy dietitians, regarding personnel engaging in unsafe or "abnormal" practices to meet physical readiness standards. For example, some personnel wait until a few weeks before the testing and then start to exercise at an intense level, while taking stimulants. While more frequent testing might reduce such behaviors, it also could make them the norm. There is also a disparity between how the Navy treats eating problems and how it treats alcohol and drug problems. While there is no structured treatment for eating disorders in the Navy, an entire department offers intensive treatment for alcohol and drug problems. There is no doubt that drug and alcohol abuse are prevalent and the treatment provided is essential, but the disparity in care should be recognized and addressed. Finally, sea-shore rotations pose challenges to maintaining physical readiness, such as access to fast food while on shore duty or having limited time to exercise due to work schedules and the pace of daily operations while at sea. The messages regarding food and weight (e.g., having McDonald's on bases, the high availability of bodybuilding products on bases) are complex and sometimes paradoxical.

Issues surrounding weight control and physical readiness are particularly salient, given the current status of U.S. military activity globally. However, the best way to choose what to change and how to change it, let alone how to implement and enforce those changes, is a source of even further debate. Any changes will inevitably generate new issues and challenges. Policy changes could have substantial economic impact by improving the health of active duty personnel, thereby reducing personnel and institutional costs associated with poor weight control and lack of physical readiness. Anthropology can play a valuable role in determining appropriate policy alternatives as well as in evaluating the result of those changes.

References Cited

Andersen, A. 1999. "Gender Related Aspects of Eating Disorders." *Journal of Gender Specific Medicine*, 2(1):47–54.

Andersen, A., L. Cohn, and T. Holbrook. 2000. *Making Weight: Men's Conflicts with Food, Weight, Shape, and Appearance*. Carlsbad, NM: Gurze.

Barker, P. 1991. *Regeneration*. New York: Penguin Books.

Binswanger, L. 1958 [1944]. "The Case of Ellen West: An Anthropological–Clinical Study." In *Existence: A New Dimension in Psychiatry and Psychology*. Rollo May, Ernest Angel and Henri F. Ellenberger, eds. Pp. 237–364. New York: Basic Books.

Bordo, S. 1993. *Unbearable Weight: Feminism, Western Culture, and the Body*. Berkeley: University of California Press.

———. 1999 *The Male Body*. New York: Farrar, Straus, and Giroux.

Brosch, L. 1998. "Physical Activity & Exercise in Active Duty Female Soldiers." Abstract from TSNRP, Funding year 1998. The Geneva Foundation.

Canguilhem, G. 1989. *The Normal and the Pathological*. New York: Zone Books.

Conway, T. L., L. J. Dutton, and P. S. Briggs. 1986. *Sailor's Perceptions of the Navy's Health and Physical Readiness Program*. NHRC Publication 86-14. AD# A171–354.

Conway T. L., L. K. Trent, and T. A. Cronan. 1989. *Navy Health and Physical Readiness Program Implementation*. NHRC Publication 89-26. AD# A223–893.

Csordas, T. 1990. "Embodiment as a Paradigm for Anthropology." *Ethos*, 18(1):6–47.

de Certeau, M. 1984. *The Practice of Everyday Life*. Berkeley: University of California Press.

DuBois, B. C. and J. D. Goodman. 1989. *Social Ecological Prediction of Obesity in U. S. Navy Personnel*. NHRC Publication 89-59.

DuBois, B. C., J. D. Goodman, and T. L. Conway. 1990. *Dietary and Behavioral Prediction of Obesity in the Navy*. NHRC Publication 89-56. AD# A223–919.

Foucault, M. 1978. *The History of Sexuality*. New York: Vintage.

Freud, S. 1960 [1901]. *The Psychopathology of Everyday Life*. New York: W. W. Norton.

Graham, W. F., L. L. Hourani, and H. Yuan. 1999. *Demographic Differences in Body Composition of Navy and Marine Corps Personnel*. NHRC Publication 99-97.

Hogdon, J. A. and E. J. Marcinik. 1983. *A Survey of Body fat Content of U. S. Navy Male Personnel*. NHRC Publication 83-4. AD# A131–500.

Hoiberg, A. S., Berard, R. H. Watten, and C. Caine. 1984. "Correlates of Weight Loss in Treatment and Follow-up." *International Journal of Obesity*, 8:457–465.

Kleinman, A. 1988. *The Illness Narratives: Suffering, Healing, and the Human Condition*. New York: Basic Books.

Lacan, J. 1977 [1966]. *Ecrits*. New York: W. W. Norton.

Marcinik, E. J., J. A. Hogdon, and J. J. O'Brien. 1985. *A Survey of Physical Training Facilities and Programs Onboard U. S. Navy Vessels*. NHRC Publication 85-26. AD# A160–654.

Marriott, B. M. ed. 1994. *Food Components to Enhance Performance: An Evaluation of Potential Performance-Enhancing Food Components for Operational Rations*. Washington D.C.: National Academy Press.

———. 1995. *Not Eating Enough: Overcoming Underconsumption of Military Operational Rations*. Washington D.C.: National Academy Press.

Mauss, M. 1973 [1934]. "Techniques of the Body." *Economy and Society*, 2:70–87.

McNulty, P. A. 1997a. "Prevalence and Contributing Factors of Eating Disorder Behaviors in Active Duty Navy Men." *Military Medicine*, 162(11):753–758.

McNulty, P. A. 1997a. "Prevalence and Contributing Factors of Eating Disorder Behaviors in a Population of Female Navy Nurses." *Military Medicine*, 162(10):703–706.

———. 2000. *Comparative Analysis of the Prevalence and Contributing Factors of Eating Disorder Behaviors Among Active Duty Army, Navy, and Air Force Service Women in the Health Care Arena, Navy Medical Center*. San Diego: U. S. Navy.

Pope, H. G., K. A. Phillips, and R. Olivardia. 2000. *The Adonis Complex: The Secret Crisis of Male Body Obsession*. New York: Free Press.

Reuters News Service. "Obesity is Increasing in the Military." *Los Angeles Times*. 2002. November 11. A35.

Scheper-Hughes, N. and M. Locke. 1987. "The Mindful Body: A Prolegomenon to Future Work in Medical Anthropology." *Medical Anthropology Quarterly*, 1(1):6–41.

Showalter, E. 1997. *Hystories: Hysterical Epidemics and Modern Culture*. New York: Columbia University Press.

Silverman, J. A. 1990. "Anorexia Nervosa in the Male: Early Historic Cases." In *Males with Eating Disorders*. A. E. Andersen, ed. Pp. 3–8. New York: Bruner/Mazel.

Stevens, L. and T. L. Conway. 1991. *Exercise and Three Psychosocial Variables: A Longitudinal Study*. NHRC Publication 91-31. AD# A250–649.

Trent, L. K. and T. L. Conway. 1988. "Dietary Factors Related to Physical Fitness Among Navy Shipboard Men." *American Journal of Health Promotion*, 3(2):12–25.

Trent, L. K. and S. L. Hurtado. 1997. *Longitudinal Trends and Gender Differences in Physical Fitness and Lifestyle Factors in the U. S. Navy (1983–1994)*. NHRC Publication 97-13. AD# A328–021.

CHAPTER 6

The Military Advisor as Warrior-King and Other "Going Native" Temptations

Anna Simons

Although anthropologists and military advisors may seem to make for strange bedfellows, they actually have more in common than meets the eye. Both spend long periods of time in the field, living with locals. Both must figure out how to establish rapport. And both are confronted by similar kinds of cross-cultural communication challenges, as well as by a host of temptations. Among the most common but also insidious of these is that of "going native," though for advisors "going native" has yet to be well defined. Clarification of this term is one goal of this chapter. A second is to point out that from the locals' perspective, of course, no advisor or anthropologist would ever be mistaken for a native. Instead, "going native" is purely a nonnative's fear—or fantasy—and can pose problems for anyone relying on an anthropologist or advisor's work. This is because members of both professions are forced to straddle two slippery slopes. On one hand, empathy can all too easily lead to sympathy, in which case any semblance of distance or objectivity is lost. On the other, being treated as a "bwana" or warrior-king can prove irresistibly seductive, and may wind up warping one's sense of mission.

We see this most starkly in the case of military advisors, though, as I will suggest, anthropologists can also suffer from a parallel form of mission creep. Thrust into what, by definition, has to be considered an ill-defined role, advisors are always in an ambiguous position. At the same time, they are never entirely powerless. Their relationship with whomever they are being tasked to advise is predicated on asymmetry; otherwise they would not be accepted as advisors in the first place. This dualism—between ambiguity and power—does not generate exactly the same dilemmas from case to case, let alone when we compare anthropologists to advisors. Advisors, for instance, almost always have more economic clout than any anthropologist can bring to bear. At the same time, they remain tethered to headquarters, no matter how removed this might be or autonomous they might feel. They must continually weigh the effects they are having. They must strive to achieve headquarters' strategic goals at the local level—a level completely removed from any most of those at headquarters are familiar with. At the same time, they must ensure that the changes they introduce are not so radical that those they are advising can not sustain them on their own. To balance such objectives does not just require, but depends on, an intimacy easily achieved by eating local food, sleeping locally, and living more like locals than like headquarters staff. But from the perspective of those not in the field, this as much as anything else often makes it seem that those *in* the field *have* "gone native."

In order to better understand what "going native" means we must first better appreciate what military advisors typically find themselves tasked and then able (or unable) to do. In what follows, I compare a series of advisory experiences to illustrate the range of constraints and opportunities that confront advisors. I conclude that whenever advisors are able to take the lead both politically *and* militarily, their position *can* go to their heads—and that this is what leads to real "going native" problems.

Advising—an Overview

Military advisors are as old as professional militaries, and though no one has studied them as a force unto themselves, they must be considered to be as integral to the development of organized warfare as any other instrument. The ancient Greeks used them, Prussia generated them, the Ottomans hired them, Chinese warlords competed with one another for their services, and today we have an entire organization in the U.S. military—the U.S. Army Special Forces—that specializes in training foreign forces. Whether explicitly, implicitly, intentionally, or unintentionally, advisors have acted as agents of change. Given such a historic role, it only stands to reason that there are distinct differences in what advising has involved over time, though not all of these differences relate to technological and organizational advances, which

are most often considered the hallmarks of military progress. More significant changes have occurred thanks to shifts in social attitude. For instance,
advice these days tends to take two forms: technical advice that might be
offered to anyone purchasing a new weapons system, to include, for example, NATO (North Atlantic Treaty Organization) allies; and training offered
to forces markedly less sophisticated than those doing the advising. To a certain extent, advice always has consisted of technical assistance and hands-on,
direct training. But the inherent inequality between those advising and those
being advised takes on a different meaning depending on whether we are
talking about noncolonial, colonial, post-, or anticolonial relations.

Colonialism is pivotal because it has long influenced attitudes toward
"natives", and because countries were either colonizers or colonized; only a
rare few escaped the experience altogether. Just beneath, and always influ-
encing, the colonial divide, meanwhile, has been the color bar. Today, both
institutions have officially disappeared. However, their legacy still influences
people's behavior and still can predetermine attitudes.

For example, if we consider the kind of advising done during the
American Revolutionary War, when French, Polish, and other experienced
officers served as observers, liaisons, and leaders, we find that these individuals volunteered their services because they believed in the American cause
(Zamoyski 1999). They were not mercenaries, since they never switched
national allegiances, continued to wear their own uniforms, and did not
serve for foreign (e.g., American) pay. Also, though they may have regarded
Americans as rubes, they clearly felt that, with improvement, Americans
could become their equals. This was clearly not the attitude, however, of
those British, French, German, and other officers sent to train troops in their
respective colonies. More often than not advisors in this situation were
placed in command. They could order, compel, coerce, and corporally pun-
ish. At the same time, over time, it was their duty to shape, guide, and—as
independence approached—mentor those under their control. Technically
speaking, no one in command should be considered an advisor. However,
individuals in positions of imperial authority helped shape a legacy that has
persisted long past independence, and continues to define expectations on
both sides of the advisor-advisee relationship. Put most bluntly, this legacy is
the conviction that locals are not to be regarded as equals. Often this idea is
drilled into individuals without their even being aware. Just consider: For
anyone schooled in imperial history (as all military officers still are), the leap
from "They were inferior, we beat them" to "They're still inferior, but they
are our equals" may be cognitively impossible. Locals, meanwhile, may
inadvertently reinforce such biases whenever they continue to model their

military, and its tactics, techniques, and procedures, on those of their former colonial masters.

Of course, emulation at the local level also can be quite conscious and instrumental. Where the state is particularly dysfunctional and the local military extortionate and/or corrupt, locals may have good reasons for wanting advisors to act and be superior. "The indigs"—it should be pointed out—are seldom gulls. They certainly are not beyond using advisors for their own political ends. Even so, a distinction must be drawn between those who seek gain from advisors whom they consider to be more than just their equals and those who regard advisors as a necessary evil. The latter, for instance, typified the Partisan attitude toward American advisors during World War II, not because there had been a prior colonial relationship between Americans and Yugoslavs, but because Marshall Tito's forces were already under communist control and in Stalin's camp (Lindsay 1993; Maclean 1950). The Partisans were happy to elicit weapons, supplies, and air support from the Allies, but were not the least bit interested in receiving training or organizational advice. The argument could be made that they were already sufficiently well trained and organized, and more adept at fighting than most of those who parachuted in to assist them. Still, a concerted enough effort was made to constrain American and British operatives that, by the end of the war, some advisors actually began to fear for their lives.

A second distinction must be drawn between skepticism or hostility directed at advisors by everyone—"who are we to need advice from *them*?"—and more individualized, personal reactions. Americans who formed guerrilla groups in Luzon (in the Philippines) during World War II experienced everything from adulation to enmity in their efforts to coordinate between the groups they led and those commanded by Filipinos (Hunt and Norling 1986; Lapham and Norling 1996; Ramsey 1990). Some of the hostility directed their way was clearly communist inspired, and some was nationalist in origin, while bandits obviously had little use for American notions of law and order. But also, in Vietnam, American advisors were unable to win over all villagers. Numerous South Vietnamese opposed any foreign presence, and pockets of recalcitrant locals made it impossible ever to fully pacify the countryside. More recently, Saudi Arabians have demonstrated considerable ambivalence toward the presence of American military personnel on Saudi soil. While some have long welcomed American training, and others barely tolerate it, still others have reacted with considerable violence, as we saw with the bombing of the Khobar Towers.

If one way to determine what influences attitudes is to ask whether we are talking about cross-cultural relations among could-be-equals, cannot-be-equals, or not-even-friends, another is to examine the dependencies inherent in who is helping whom with what. By doing so we also discover just how difficult it is to distinguish between constraints inherent in the physical operating environment and those that are more social or inter-personal in origin.

Constraints (and Opportunities): Franklin Lindsay and Ben Malcom

Security has to be considered the number one priority of advisors, whether in peacetime or during war. In a hostile environment security is clearly the paramount concern, though what comprises security depends on where exactly advisors and advisees are located. If they are behind enemy lines in an uninhabited area, their safety is largely up to them and depends on their field craft (how well hidden they can stay), military skills (how much firepower they can bring to bear), and supply situation (how long they can last without resupply). The situation is complicated if there are civilians nearby, and it becomes trickier still if the advisor(s)/advisees must rely on locals for food, transportation, intelligence, and other essentials. Then they have a vulnerability over which they can exert little, if any, control, and maintaining local rapport becomes critical. However, more is required than just acting friendly. To ensure that their existence and/or location is not exposed, advisors and their advisees must offer locals something that the locals otherwise cannot provide for themselves. Ironically enough, this is usually security—in the form of law and order and protecting communities from bandits and bullies.

The advisor–advisee local relationship is paradoxical in a number of ways and reveals a series of interlocking dependencies. Initially, advisors are always most dependent. Over time, if they are good, they can turn this situation around. For example, if advisors—particularly single advisors—get sick or are injured, their lives directly depend on advisees and/or locals nursing them back to health. Yet advisors themselves are regarded as sources of (Western) medical knowledge and often bring with them or can acquire medications and first aid treatments that are locally unknown or unavailable. This also can be true for food, especially when advisors can call for resupply by air. Then they can ask for large quantities of staples, such as rice, to augment local food supplies (Hilsman 1990; Peers and Brelis 1963). Although advisors have little choice but to rely on whatever the locals use for shelter or warmth, they provide access to goods that locals may think they need more: guns, ammunition, radios, and so on. Communications is another realm in which advisors are caught both being dependent—sometimes messages can be passed only via the local net—and in command—with their radios they instantaneously plug themselves, their advisees, and the locals into a wider world.

By now it should be clear: The advisory relationship is just like any other exchange relationship. Members on each side must feel they are mutually benefiting for the relationship to last, though the advisor is always more beholden first. Also, because the arrangements for an advisor to be present are made at higher command levels, the relationship can stay lopsided in the field, where the advisor is sent whether the locals are receptive or not. The most effective advisors invariably intuit how to turn constraints into opportunities. In some situations this is easier than in others, especially when we consider that advisors whose mission it is to help *establish* an armed force from scratch face a very different set of challenges from those who are joining a unit or force that is already up and running. This situation was made more than apparent during World War II. In the Asian theater, for instance, advisors were often responsible for recruiting and training guerrilla forces (in Burma, the Philippines, even China). They designed and helped lead these forces, acting as teachers, trainers, coordinators, liaisons, and conduits. In contrast, advisors in Europe tended to be sent in as liaisons, but more often functioned simply as conduits and were primarily (and sometimes only) valued for what they could bring in via air drops.

Even this constrained role could be used for leverage, but only if the advisor on the ground was willing to take certain risks. Here it is instructive to consider the experiences of Franklin Lindsay, who was parachuted into Slovenia in 1944 to help destroy a series of rail links (Lindsay 1993). The Partisans didn't have the supplies, or the exact know-how, to do this on their own; however, Marshall Tito also turned out to be much less interested in slowing a Nazi withdrawal through Slovenia than he was in extracting arms, explosives, and other material out of the deal in order to fight rival Yugoslav forces. In the end, even Lindsay admits he did more for the Partisans than they did for the Allied cause. Given the set-up of the relationship, this probably could not be helped, but Lindsay never fully used the leverage he had to stall (or stop) air drops. Instead, he worried that if he tried to compel the Partisans too often they would have him removed; thus he routinely stopped himself short. Compounding his problems was the fact that he never became proficient in Slovenian. At most, he could sense that he was being manipulated; the Partisans definitely kept him on a tight leash. But had he possessed better passive listening skills, he might have understood sooner and more completely the ways in which he and his fellow advisors were being used, and could have made the case more forcefully to his superiors that the Partisans were not to be trusted and that perhaps their rivals, the Chetniks, should not have been so quickly dismissed.

Advisors are always used. They tend to do much better when they understand this at the outset and then employ *how* they are being used to their advantage. Without question, the more culturally and politically attuned individuals are going in to a situation, the easier it is for them to react appropriately. But sometimes, too, this is simply a matter of being able to read other people, regardless of regional expertise. Take, for instance, Ben Malcom (1996). As a young infantry lieutenant with no previous experience in Asia (or unconventional warfare), he was faced with a classic advisory dilemma within weeks of reaching the field. In this case, the "field" was a small island off the coast of North Korea in 1952. There Malcom was assigned to help train a partisan unit whose previous Korean commander had been assassinated. Malcom's American superiors were not sure whether they could trust Mr. Pak, the unit's new commander. Mr. Pak, meanwhile, asked Malcom to accompany him on a brief visit to his safe area on the North Korean mainland, someplace both men knew Malcom was not supposed to visit. Was this a set-up? To earn Mr. Pak's trust, Malcom had little choice but to proceed; he realized, in the moment during which he was forced to decide whether to trust Mr. Pak, that he really could not refuse if he hoped to succeed as an advisor. Indeed, a whole series of interlocking dependencies manifested themselves. For instance, although it was Mr. Pak's trustworthiness that concerned the Americans, Mr. Pak needed to measure Malcom's worth because it was really up to Malcom to determine how Mr. Pak would be perceived. And, in fact, once they returned from this trip, with a bond established, Malcom's self-appointed next task *was* to convince his superiors of Mr. Pak's credibility. He did this by suggesting and then having Mr. Pak help plan and execute a daring raid. Of course, the fact that the raid called for naval and air support that only Malcom could coordinate for the Partisans certainly did not hurt his standing in their eyes. In fact, everyone benefited from this particular military action, and it took place early enough in Malcom's tour that he was able to capitalize on it, and its effects, immediately.

Malcom, then, made the most of his situation. Lindsay did not. At first glance this might seem surprising, since, on paper, one might think Malcom was no better, and in some regards was less, qualified than Lindsay to be an advisor: He was not Ivy League-educated, spoke no foreign languages, felt no particular affinity for North Koreans, and did not seek the assignment. Yet he quickly did a superlative job; he cared—how much he cared we will see shortly. As for why Lindsay did not care as much, we have to consider the fact that Lindsay was fighting *alongside* and Malcom was fighting *against* communists. Thus Lindsay was working with people whose ultimate goals were not the same as his, whereas Malcom and the North Korean Partisans were fighting together for Koreans' freedom. This fact as much as anything may have helped set the parameters for what Malcom felt he *could* and Lindsay felt he *couldn't* do. Other factors to take into account were that Malcom lived with his Partisans on an island and felt relatively secure. He was less consistently dependent on them than Lindsay was on his Partisans, who were forced (along with Lindsay) to stay on the move. Still, while differences in the setting, location, and even timing of events clearly shaped each man's approach—as did differences in their personalities—the ultimate constraint appears to have been their reception: What the Partisans were willing to accept from Lindsay was far more limited than what the North Koreans were willing to accept from Malcom. Lindsay could offer no advice. Malcom could offer military advice, and eagerly did so at the operational, tactical, and strategic levels.

As for going native, neither man did, though perhaps it is better to draw the distinction between these two this way: Lindsay was not the least bit tempted, and Malcom had no need. The North Koreans accepted him just as he was. They themselves comprised a relatively isolated military unit, with no nearby villagers to have to worry about and thus no local politics to ensnare them—or, consequently, him.

Opportunities (and Constraints): T. E. Lawrence, Edward Lansdale, and John Paul Vann

Not so T. E. Lawrence (Asher 1998; Lawrence 1963 [1926]; Mack 1998 [1976]) or Edward Lansdale (Curry 1998; Lansdale 1991), who became behind-the-scenes politicians bar none. In one respect, the experiences of these two archetypal advisors were exactly like those of Lindsay and Malcom. In none of these cases did any of these men receive specific guidance. Here, for instance, were Lindsay's orders: "Major Lindsay is appointed Commanding Officer of the Allied Military Mission to the Partisan forces in the Stajerska area. As such, he is fully empowered to represent the Allied Military Authorities in this area. He or his delegate is the sole representative of Brigadier Maclean and through him of the Allied Commanders-in-Chief, on all matters which involve liaison with Partisan Military Authorities in the Stajerska, including military plans and supplies" (Lindsey 1993:29).

Compare this with how Lieutenant Colonel Edward Lansdale describes the mission statement he received: "My orders were plain. The United States government wanted me to give all help feasible to the Philippine government in stopping the attempt by the Communist-led Huks to overthrow that government by force. My help was to consist mainly of advice where needed and desired. It was up to me to figure out how best to do this" (Lansdale 1991:2).

The most significant difference between Lansdale and Lawrence on one hand and Lindsay and Malcom on the other is the levels at which they operated. Lansdale and Lawrence offered political and not just military advice. And both did so at operational, tactical, *and* strategic levels. Both men also became kingmakers. This is not what either was specifically told to do, but it is what each man was positioned to be able to do, and each capitalized on the opportunity in his own way. No one, for instance, told Lawrence that he should turn Faisal into the leader of the Arab revolt. Similarly, it was Lansdale who helped decide that the United States should back Ramon Magsaysay. While Lawrence clearly saw something pliable in Faisal, Lansdale concentrated on what was most promising in Magsaysay—namely that here was someone already committed to reforming both the Filipino military and government. Lansdale suggested various ways in which Magsaysay, as minister of defense, could use the military to bolster, protect, and extend democracy, which would in turn convince Filipinos that the army was *their* army and on their side. He did this through a series of nonstop conversations with Magsaysay during which he also consciously fed the man's personal ambitions.

In some regards, Lawrence's task was much more straightforward than Lansdale's, since Faisal (his chief advisee) was already well known and well respected before Lawrence ever arrived on the scene. Faisal, as a sharif, was a member of the "ruling" family of Mecca, and he, his father, and his brothers had long contemplated Arab independence from the Ottomans. What Lawrence had to help him do was unite the various Bedouin tribes outside his immediate circle of followers and then keep widening this circle of support to break the Ottoman hold on Arabia. Even more important, Lawrence had to keep money and materiel pouring into Faisal's coffers, which meant retaining British support for what many in England considered to be only a sideshow. With World War I being fought in the trenches in Europe—and with one failed sideshow in Gallipoli already—Lawrence had to make more of both Faisal and the Arab revolt than either perhaps merited. At the same time, to do what he wanted without too much oversight or interference required him to keep certain of his intentions secret and to willfully ignore or avoid receiving messages from his superiors that ran counter to his plans. In this sense, Lawrence clearly put his intentions ahead of his government's intent and can be said to have strayed "off the reservation" at least some of the time. Does this mean he went native? Many would argue yes.

Yet what then of Lansdale? Lansdale was always accused of the opposite, of being "the quiet American" who was able to do his government's secret bidding.

On the face of it, and given their operating environments, Lawrence's and Lansdale's styles could not have been more different. Lawrence dressed like a Bedouin, lived like a Bedouin, rode camels like a Bedouin, and operated in Arabic. Lansdale never dressed or lived like a Filipino. Yet, on closer examination, many of their methods for how they advised were eerily similar. For one, Lawrence shadowed Faisal as much as possible, just as Lansdale did Magsaysay. This enabled each of them to prime their respective advisees and interject ideas and shape projects that both leaders could then present (and self-present) as their own. The intimacy with which Lawrence and Lansdale made sure they operated offers a sharp and ultimately telling contrast to the methods employed by John Paul Vann, arguably the most famous American advisor in Vietnam, and someone who was aware of both Lawrence and Lansdale (Sheehan 1988). Like Lawrence and Lansdale, Vann also set himself up to be a kingmaker, but unlike them, Vann failed.[1]

Lieutenant Colonel John Paul Vann's advisory assignment was to put together a coordinated war effort in the northern part of the Mekong Delta. The counterpart he was given was Colonel Huynh Van Cao. With no choice but to work with or through Cao, Vann was constrained from the outset. At the same time, though, Vann did not do what Lawrence and Lansdale did. They steeped themselves in local politics to better understand their situation. Vann assessed his situation strictly militarily. He was a gifted tactician and strategist who understood exactly why American and South Vietnamese forces were so ineffective at the operational and tactical levels, and—militarily—knew exactly how to fix the problem. One thing he was convinced he had to do was get Cao to fight. Indeed, his self-proclaimed goal was to turn Cao into "the Tiger of South Vietnam" (Sheehan 1988:75). Unfortunately, in his desperation to bring out the fighter in Cao, Vann ignored Cao the politician and remained blind to the political constraints that prevented Cao from doing what Vann wanted. In Cao's own calculus, he could afford to become just enough of a hero to garner favor with President Ngo Dinh Diem, but he should never be too successful for fear that Diem would then view him as a rival and a threat. Unlike Lawrence or Lansdale, who tried to view things through the natives' eyes, Vann never attempted to assess Cao's situation as Cao might. Worse, in giving public credit to Cao for operations he (Vann) planned, Vann made it impossible to later claim, even to his own chain of command, that Cao was not as effective as advertised. Vann basically boxed himself in.

More tragically still, despite Vann's inability to appreciate why corruption was so rampant in South Vietnam, or why members of the Army of the

Republic of Viet Nam (ARVN) would not fight harder, he clearly understood that the United States would lose if it did not change its strategy and tactics. He tried to make this clear to his superiors, as well as to policymakers in the Department of Defense, but for a host of reasons never managed to get through. This, then, makes for another striking contrast with Lansdale and Lawrence, who both succeeded as advisors in no small measure because they excelled at convincing their superiors to listen to them. Not only can Lawrence and Lansdale be said to have operated politically *and* militarily in Arabia and the Philippines, but they were consummate strategists in London and Washington as well. Both were well connected at the highest levels. More to the point still, both were considered to be *the* authorities on cross-cultural relations in the region of the world in which they were operating. Lawrence, it should be noted, also perfected the art of *appearing* the expert. Lansdale was the former advertising executive, but Lawrence is the one who made sure he looked as if he had gone native, which he did in part to advertise how well he knew "his" natives; there was no other reason to appear at headquarters, for instance, in Bedouin garb.

Had Vann tried to pull something like that off, it, too, would have back-fired. Not only did Vietnam require a different kind of irregular warfare to be fought in the halls of power than that called for by the Arab revolt or the Huk rebellion, but Vann was too high-ranking in too prominent a position. At the same time, he was not singular enough; there were numerous other advisors of his rank, tasked with similar assignments. Lawrence and Lansdale were ones of a kind. Ironically, in Vietnam the more junior or remotely located advisors tended to better fit at least this half of the Lawrence-Lansdale mold. No matter how forsaken they may have felt by their own chain of command, and no matter how little political clout they had with their superiors, it was lieutenants, captains, and noncommissioned officers who were perfectly positioned to develop empathy. Also, they were the individuals who had locals there to remind them on a daily basis just how important they were in *their* scheme of things. Americans who took advantage of this wound up doing exactly what Lansdale would have had all Americans do to win a people's war: They engaged *with* the people, at the grassroots. Here, though, in the worst of the hardship postings, is also where the temptations to go native invariably proved most seductive.

Going Native (or Not) in Two Acts: David Donovan and Alan Cornett

Not only did being and feeling isolated afford advisors all sorts of leeway in terms of dress, comportment, and attitude in Vietnam, but isolation also presented them with choices. At one end of the range of possibilities, they could hunker down and wait out their tours, making little local impact. Alternatively, they could attempt to raise the standard of living for as many people as possible within their area of operation. For those who took the latter approach, nights were often spent setting up raids and ambushes designed to flush out the Vietcong, while days were devoted to improving local sanitation, running clinics, setting up (and supplying) local schools, and training and inspiring locals to want to take over these and other jobs (cf. Hickey 1965; West 1972).

A general rule seemed to be: The more effective the team, the more the locals asked of it, while there was no good way to be effective without becoming enmeshed in local politics. Here is how First Lieutenant David Donovan describes his situation in 1968:

I was a twenty-three-year-old idealistic young army officer, left essentially alone to fight my own little war with my own little team of companions. I was determined and eager to do my best. Given free rein by a do-nothing but compliant district chief, I began to accept a growing list of duties and responsibilities. Military operations were performed as I directed; people were imprisoned or freed at my word; food and clothing from various agencies were distributed where I said, when I said; aircraft bombed or strafed at my command; curfews were established according to my wishes; villagers applied to or through me for medical help, school, supplies, building materials, and agricultural development assistance. I could even cause the summary execution of practically anyone in my district. In many ways I controlled life and death of thousands of the people.

The Vietnamese recognized the power I wielded, and after a while I began to expect the almost fawning courtesy with which I was treated. With no one around to give me my true measure, I began to accept my elevated status, and I began to use the powers in my hands as if they were mine by right.

Most of the responsibilities were not truly mine, but I knew the district chief would approve anything I did, and if I didn't do it, I had the definite impression that very little would get done. Perhaps it was only youthful American arrogance that made me take these powers that were outside my rightful reach, perhaps it was the almost mystical idealism with which I took on my whole task, but when I had the chance to get something done I by-God took it! Perhaps I was just a high-toned American, but in my dreams I was a cavalier for freedom, I was a warrior for Camelot. Even more than that. I was a Warrior King. (Donovan 1985:127)

Donovan is worth quoting at such length for two reasons: He understood the power inherent in his position and the predicament in which this placed him. Also, he exemplifies what someone is capable of when he can offer political and military advice at the operational, tactical, and strategic levels: He leads, he no longer just advises. This is substantively different from the positions Lansdale and Lawrence occupied as kingmakers. As much as they, too, collapsed together political and military advice and offered operational, tactical, and strategic assistance, they never took charge. Also, no matter how "native" Lawrence may have looked to his fellow Brits, we must remember that no one in Arabia mistook him for someone in authority. It is arguable whether any Arabs even viewed him as *an* authority, let alone a subject matter expert on what he has since been credited with codifying: guerrilla warfare. Yet there is no question that Donovan, who clearly was not any more knowledgeable about the local situation than any of the Vietnamese he worked with, *was* in command. What helped elevate him was the fact that he not only thought in terms of the good of the community but acted accordingly. Meanwhile, the more he was able to do, the more in charge people wanted him to be. He managed this, as far as we know, without abusing his power. He also did it having adopted the dress, diet, and mannerisms of the local villagers. He was even initiated into the Hoa Hao religious sect. Outwardly he must have appeared deeply sympathetic. But does this mean he went native?

The answer has to be no on two counts. First, though Donovan's attitudes were clearly colored by his team's isolation and the fact that he was far more comfortable living like a Vietnamese than an American, he never once deviated from prosecuting the war exactly as he was supposed to fight it, in terms of denying the area to the North Vietnamese and Vietcong sympathizers. It helped that, in being ignored, he found himself with tremendous leeway. But nothing that he did ran counter to larger war aims. In this sense, no contradictions arose between his commitment to the local community and his loyalty to the United States—and "his" villagers' cause *could* become his own. Unlike Lawrence, Donovan never had to gamble that what he was doing *for* the Vietnamese might work, even though it flew in the face of his own government's aims. The argument also can be made, of course, that by taking on the role of warrior-king, Donovan really was not acting very Vietnamese.[2] Instead, by accepting (or carving out) this position, he retained just enough distance from his "subjects" that there could be no mistaking him for one of them.

Oddly enough, it is this status differential that brings us closest to the real crux of the "going native" problem. In none of the advisory literature is there ever a hint that an advisor might have wanted to be mistaken *for* a native. Instead, advisors always want to be treated as at least slightly better than the natives—or, at the very least, as a first among equals. Whether this is what they go into advising expecting and thus work toward, or this is how they are received and then is what they come to expect, depends on the historical context (e.g., is the relationship noncolonial, postcolonial, etc.). But also, as alluded to earlier, paternalism may simply be inherent in any relationship in which advisors are assigned to train forces that are not well outfitted, lack basic infantry skills, and live in harsh conditions. Rudimentary settings themselves may make it far easier for advisors to want to lead and not just guide or assist. At the same time, on multiple levels, this is likely to not only reinforce but reward their sense of their own superiority. If this idea is not then tempered by respect for local ways of doing things—and this is an extremely difficult balance to maintain over time, as Donovan poignantly admits—such individuals may well wind up acting too imperial, or, worse, they may begin to try to out-primitive the primitives. Of course, the real horror is when they appear to do both, as Francis Ford Coppola would have us believe Kurtz does in Joseph Conrad's *Heart of Darkness*. Yet even in *Apocalypse Now* (never mind Conrad's novel), we must remember Kurtz's power over the natives rests in his *not* being a native. At most, what we can say is that Kurtz takes to the situation as if *it*—the situation—were natural; it appeals to his most elemental (or primitive) self. What we then mistake for his having gone native *with* the natives is really his going native in the moment. Clearly, both book and movie represent fictionalized accounts of what it means to go native, and Coppola's character is the only one of the two who can be considered to have been an advisor. Nevertheless, this preference for living large in a liminal situation—namely war—does seduce advisors. We see this most clearly if we compare Sergeant Alan Cornett's account of his experiences in Vietnam with Donovan's now-classic memoir (Cornett 2000).

Like Donovan, Cornett served on a MAT (mobile advisory) team in 1968, though one immediate difference between the two is that Donovan served a single tour. By choice, Cornett spent seven years "in-country." Ergo the title of his book, *Gone Native*. At several points in his memoir he describes feeling more comfortable in Vietnam than in the United States. Not only was it "the only world that would accept me for who I was" (p. 175), but "even today I don't feel the same level of security and comfort I had there" (p. 204). Cornett describes himself as having "gone so native that I would shun fellow Americans because they didn't understand my relationship with the people. I didn't like the way many Americans treated the

Vietnamese, as if they were a second-class people in their own land" (p. 249). From this excerpt it might sound as if Cornett was fully committed to helping the Vietnamese in the same manner as Donovan. He certainly could have; he was trained and previously worked as a Special Forces medic. But by the time he feels most at ease he is working for the Phoenix Program, whose sole purpose was to neutralize members of the Vietcong infrastructure.

Cornett's account is revealing on two counts. Like Lawrence, Lansdale, Malcom, and Donovan, he gets caught up in the moment. But unlike them, he is less absorbed by what he is doing *for* people (e.g., the people of South Vietnam) than by what he can do *to* the Vietcong. He also does not seem to want this moment to end. Over time, it is clear, war becomes his preferred environment; its elemental rules make sense, even if the politics do not. In fact, by the end, it would appear to be less Vietnam that he finds so comfortable as his status in the war zone, where he serves with an elite unit and is one of only a handful of Americans to routinely accompany a hard core group of Vietnamese. His fellow combatants are the people who matter most to him. Something else that emerges is that his loyalties do not shift so much as they clarify over time. He cares about himself first. Second come friends from whichever unit he is serving with, and then, once he marries the sister of one of these friends, comes his wife. Although she, as well as his brother-in-law, are both Vietnamese, this still does not change his fundamental orientation. His connections to them pull him deeper into their circle. They also contribute to how conflicted he sometimes feels. But his response is more personalized than it is dogmatic: He feels bad, he gets angry, he lashes out. From time to time he even questions policy. But he never seeks to make it for himself in the field. Unlike Donovan (or Vann), he does not strive to change the local situation. Instead, he finds a niche and revels in it. In a strange sort of way, this makes Cornett no less effective than Donovan, but for a very different kind of mission. What it also means, though, is that Cornett no more goes native in the way he imagines he did than did anyone else.

Staying True

What defines going native? For observers, the most obvious warning signs lie in appearance. Most militaries are predicated on a tight linkage between appearance and attitude, or rectitude and comportment—thus, the significance of looks as an indicator. However, the problem in advisory situations is that looks can easily deceive. In fact, this is exactly what they are often meant to do. For instance, Lawrence was quite forthright that no Bedouin would mistake him for one of them; his aim in dressing like one was largely to fool anyone who might identify him as a Brit from a distance. By obscuring his identity this way he was actually following in a long line of Englishmen who attempted to pass through hostile regions dressed as natives, but always as natives from somewhere else. Richard Burton, the first European to live to write about his penetration of Mecca, accomplished this by pretending to be a merchant from a region completely removed from any he was traveling through (cf. Lovell 1998). Likewise, British agents sent to secretly map Central Asia often posed as locally credible itinerants (cf. Meyer and Brysac 1999). Of course, there were always other reasons, beyond not wanting to stand out, for agents and advisors to don native dress, comfort chief among them. Regardless, changing one's looks in the field has almost always been done for instrumental reasons. It is *persisting* in those appearances outside of a field situation that should set off alarms. Then a modified, unkempt, or absent uniform represents the surest sign that all is not as it once was. An advisor may be defying military convention just to make the point that he is different from those in the rear or at headquarters. He could be signaling that he is the expert (as Lawrence seemed to) or that his work is dirtier, harder, and more important than theirs. This was certainly advisors' attitude in Vietnam, where individuals regularly took pride in looking as if they had just come in from "the bush."

Without question, there is always a certain mystique that someone who has spent time in a hardship posting can wrap around himself. Having endured hardships with teammates and locals makes for emotional bonds that those who have been in such positions feel no one who has not can understand.[3] The fact, too, that advisors like Donovan and Malcom were living much the same life as those they were advising clearly led them to align themselves with their advisees. One could make the case that an advisor cannot be effective unless he can see the world as those he is advising see it. Certainly Lawrence's and Lansdale's abilities to do so contributed to their success, while Lindsay's and Vann's failures to do so led to innumerable problems. Having said this, though, empathy is not—or should it be allowed to become—sympathy; just because it helps when advisors understand what others feel does not mean they would do even better by *feeling* what their advisees feel. Empathy is difficult enough. Advisors often realize that their country's long-term interests are not necessarily the same as those of the country they are in. If they care enough about the people they have been tasked to advise, they may think, though, that not only do they know better than their superiors, but they must do better, too. This is what should most worry any chain of command, especially since an advisor's loyalties will remain invisible *unless* he wears them on his sleeve.

As far as advisors' commanders are concerned, their value lies in their ability to liaise, coordinate, and gather intelligence. Ideally, advisors' efforts with indigenous forces should dovetail, support, and augment the main effort, which—at least in wartime—generally involves harassing, tying down and diverting, and denying support to the enemy. At a minimum, we can say that those responsible for sending advisors, and the commanders of indigenous forces who agree to accept them, share the same foe. Ideally, too, they should share the same war aims. But, in reality, they seldom do. Nor do war aims have to be completely congruent for there to be agreements to send and receive advisors.

Here then is where we find the ultimate source of friction, anxiety, and frustration for advisors in the field. No matter how difficult the pas de deux between forces proves to be at higher/strategic command or even diplomatic levels, advisors are the ones who have to live the contradictions on the ground, on a daily basis, and then must continue living with them afterward. This proves psychically costly, as T. E. Lawrence describes over and over again in *Seven Pillars of Wisdom*. Lawrence knew the Arabs were fighting for freedom from foreign rule. At times he even seemed to consider their cause more his creation than theirs. But he also knew the British and French were not about to give up their suzerainty in the Middle East—and it was a British uniform he wore, British pay he drew, and British adulation he ultimately sought.

Given Lawrence's penchant for fictionalization and his deeply conflicted nature, it is hard to know just how badly he felt he had betrayed the sharifs.[4] This is much easier to gauge in other cases. Nelson Miles, for instance, commanding officer of the Sino-American Cooperative Organization (SACO), was quite impassioned about the fact that the United States sold its wartime allies, the nationalist Chinese, down the river after World War II (Miles 1950). Although Miles fought innumerable battles on the nationalists' behalf in Washington, his conscience suffered long afterward as a result of U.S. policy (Miles 1967). Malcom, who only recently has been allowed to publicly discuss his Korean War experiences, has been stumping hard to make up for years of classified silence. He also has been fighting to attain public recognition for the North Korean partisans he fought with whom both we and the South Koreans, essentially abandoned (Ben Malcom, personal communication: 11/8/01). Special Forces soldiers who participated in Operation Provide Comfort in northern Iraq, just a decade ago, still speak bitterly about what they regard as the United States' betrayal of the Kurds. In fact, many Special Forces officers and soldiers now accept the fact that they are rarely sent abroad just to assist another military; they recognize that when the

United States has gotten what it needs the relationship is finished, never mind whether those on the receiving end have gotten everything they were promised.[5] Still, no matter how they rationalize it, *living* this is painful. Being made to quit before the situation on the ground merits quitting is not only disillusioning but can cause long-term emotional damage. It proves especially difficult given power flows that make advisors feel responsible *for* and not just *to*.

Anthropologists through the Looking Glass

As murky as an advisory situation can be, anthropologists would seem to have it tougher going in (more choices), but easier moving on (less power). What do I mean? We swear no allegiances, take no oath, and have no chain of command. We choose our own fieldwork sites, our own problems, and our own supervisors. There is nothing that we *have* to do. There are certain things we should not do. For instance, our one clear ethical rule is to do no harm. Or, to put this in more positive terms: We should conduct research according to the golden rule, treating others only as we would want to be treated ourselves. If we follow this, then our responsibilities to the people we study should be congruent with our responsibilities to those we study them for. Indeed, if we apply the golden rule, we should be thinking about both groups as if they are one. However, it also can be argued that anyone who thinks that this is how s/he operates is as self-deluding as Sergeant Cornett. That is because we, much like advisors, engage in an exchange relationship with locals whenever we conduct fieldwork. We seek to gain data, information, knowledge, and, ideally, understanding about some other way of life. What do we offer in exchange? Sometimes we are able to pay people money or we give them gifts. Otherwise, we may help them practice their English and serve as entertainment. Invariably, when asked why we do what we do, we say something like "So people who don't understand what your lives are like can better appreciate you." This is the truth as we fervently believe it, but by saying this we are also leading people to believe that they will receive some intangible benefit from our research later on and that this will be as useful to them as something concrete in the here and now.

Contrast this with what advisors offer. Often advisors, too, promise more than they can deliver—especially since, seeing what they have, people routinely expect them to be able to provide more than they possibly can. Even so, advisors are doers. If they are allowed to, they can build or demolish things, heal or hurt people, and teach and train new skills. We—as anthropologists—just extract information and, at most, interpret between cultures. Or, at least, that is what we are limited to doing if we intend to stay empathic and unbiased. If not, we can become advocates.

For all the reasons already given, however, we no more can become natives than advisors can. Adopted members of a tribe, fictive kin—yes. But a native as far as the natives are concerned—never. Nor can we think like natives and remain anthropologists, unless the natives we study are ourselves. That leaves us with advocacy, although it is not clear that we have any right to really speak *for* anyone either. Ironically, this brings us much closer to military advisors' bind than most anthropologists might like to admit. Although as recently as Vietnam, advisors in some places could still think *for* the locals— Donovan, for instance, could, though Vann could not—that was already three decades ago. People everywhere in the world have only grown more self-aware. Consider Operation Focus Relief, the recent effort by the United States to have Special Forces soldiers "train" seven battalions of West African peacekeepers, thereby sensitizing them to human rights abuses: "Nigerians welcomed the proffered equipment but bristled at training. Citing their greater combat experience, they saw little to gain from U.S. instruction" (Leatherwood 2001/2002:81).

No population appears to be as unsophisticated or as naïve as we once could assume people to be. Nor do people elsewhere seem quite so willing to accept the exchanges we suggest for the reasons we give. Of course, the argument can be—and has been—made that no one ever did (cf. Asad [ed.] 1973; Marcus and Fischer 1986). Politics are inherent in all exchanges. Without question, too, the most effective military advisors have always recognized this and have used their status as non-natives to distinct advantage. Can the same be said for anthropologists? Absolutely. For decades now, the discipline has recognized the significance of power flows and the extent to which ethnographers consciously or unconsciously avail themselves of them. But despite our *intellectually* acknowledging this, we are still easily seduced by the fantasy: There is probably not an anthropologist among us who, in venturing to the field for the first (or even second or third) time, does not want to be the exception. Who among us does not want to be considered at one with *our* people? If not inherent in those of us who choose to be anthropologists, this desire may simply be part and parcel of what we do. After all, even if we can not get the natives to buy us as one of them, this is certainly how we vie to be regarded by one another, proving once again that positioning is everything and being looked up to as knowing more is best of all.

Notes

Having taught my military advisor class five times, I owe much to all the officers who have passed through it, many of whom have served or are serving as advisors themselves; to Joe Andrade, who served as an advisor in El Salvador and has always advised me (and our students) about advising; to Lee Edwards, who served as an advisor in Vietnam and whose discussions about his experiences and comments on this chapter serve as a reminder that I am barely scratching the surface.

1. Here it should be noted that Lansdale, on a subsequent assignment, failed to get South Vietnam's president, Ngo Dinh Diem, to substantively reform his government—a mission he was given by the U.S. government after his success in the Philippines. However, unlike Magsaysay, Diem was already in power. Thus, Lansdale was not in the role of kingmaker. Worse, he had to compete for Diem's attention with other advisors (both American and French).
2. For what it meant to act or be Vietnamese, see Jamieson (1993).
3. These are the same sort of sentiments, at a much broader level, that account for many combat veterans' membership in associations like the American Legion, the VFW, and the like.
4. Michael Asher convincingly demonstrates that portions of Lawrence's *Seven Pillars* are fictionalized.
5. This is well described in the final pages of Shachochis (1999).

References Cited

Asad, Talal. ed. 1973. *Anthropology and the Colonial Encounter*. New York: Humanities Press.

Asher, Michael. 1998. *Lawrence: The Uncrowned King of Arabia*. Woodstock, NY: Overlook Press.

Cornett, Alan. 2000. *Gone Native: An NCO's Story*. New York: Ballantine.

Currey, Cecil. 1998. *Edward Lansdale: The Unquiet American*. Washington, D.C.: Brassey's.

Donovan, David. 1985. *Once a Warrior King: Memories of an Officer in Vietnam*. New York: McGraw-Hill.

Hickey, G. C. 1965. *The American Military Advisor and His Foreign counterpart: The Case of Vietnam*. Santa Monica, CA: RAND.

Hilsman, Roger. 1990. *American Guerrilla: My War Behind Japanese Lines*. Washington, DC: Brassey's.

Hunt, Ray, and Bernard Norling. 1986. *Behind Jap Lines: An American Guerrilla in the Philippines*. Lexington: University Press of Kentucky.

Jamieson, Neil. 1993. *Understanding Vietnam*. Berkeley: University of California Press.

Lansdale, Edward. 1991. *In the Midst of Wars: An American's Mission to Southeast Asia*. New York: Fordham University Press.

Lapham, Robert, and Bernard Norling. 1996. *Lapham's Raiders: Guerrillas in the Philippines 1942–1945*. Lexington: University Press of Kentucky.

Lawrence, T. E. 1963 [1926]. *Seven Pillars of Wisdom*. New York: Dell.

Leatherwood, D. G. 2001/2002. "Peacekeeping in West Africa." *Joint Force Quarterly*. Autumn–Winter. P. 29.

Lindsay, Franklin. 1993. *Beacons in the Night: With the OSS and Tito's Partisans in Wartime Yugoslavia*. Stanford, CA: Stanford University Press.

Lovell, Mary. 1998. *A Rage to Live: A Biography of Richard and Isabel Burton*. New York: W. W. Norton.

Mack, John. 1998 [1976]. *A Prince of Our Disorder: The Life of T. E. Lawrence*. Cambridge, MA: Harvard University Press.

Maclean, Fitzroy. 1950. *Escape to Adventure*. Boston: Little, Brown.

Malcom, Ben. 1996. *White Tigers: My Secret War in North Korea*. Washington, D.C.: Brassey's.

Marcus, George, and Michael Fischer. 1986. *Anthropology as Cultural Critique: An Experimental Moment in the Human Sciences*. Chicago: University of Chicago Press.

Meyer, Karl E. and Shareen Blair Brysac. 1999. *Tournament of Shadows: The Great Game and the Race for Empire in Central Asia*. Washington, D.C.: Counterpoint.

Miles, Nelson. 1950. "Foreword". In *SACO: Rice Paddy Navy*. Roy Stratton, ed. Pp. xi–xvi. Pleasantville, NY: C.S. Palmer.

——. 1967. *A Different Kind of War: The Little-Known Story of the Combined forces Created in China by the U.S. Navy and the Chinese During World War II*. Garden City, NY: Doubleday.

Peers, William and Dean Brelis. 1963. *Behind the Burma Road: The Story of America's Most Successful Guerrilla Force*. Boston: Little, Brown.

Ramsey, Edwin. 1990. *Lieutenant Ramsey's War: From Horse Soldier to Guerrilla Commander*. Washington, D.C.: Brassey's.

Shachochis, Robert. 1999. *The Immaculate Invasion*. New York: Viking.

Sheehan, Neil. 1988. *A Bright Shining Lie: John Paul Vann and America in Vietnam*. New York: Random House.

West, F. J. Jr. 1972. *The Village*. New York: Harper & Row.

Zamoyski, Adam. 1999. *Holy Madness: Romantics, Patriots, and Revolutionaries, 1776–1871*. New York: Viking.

CHAPTER 7

Integrating Diversity and Understanding the Other at the U.S. Naval Academy

Clementine Fujimura

Introduction

The modern military has traditionally embraced scientific development and technological innovation as keys to superiority and victory in warfare. The curriculum of the U.S. Naval Academy reflects this philosophy by focusing on the so-called hard-sciences, such as engineering, thereby excluding subjects such as anthropology. Qualitative studies in general have taken a backseat to quantitative studies. This chapter discusses the culture behind attitudes held by traditionalists at the Naval Academy toward course offerings in cultural studies and anthropology. Responses to cultural studies have included skepticism and cynicism, connoting a general disdain for the study of ethos and emotion and of cultural and individual diversity. Stereotyped as "softer," cultural studies are expected by midshipmen to be easy courses. Moreover, these "less rigorous" sciences were, in the past, not considered important. However, as today's military grapples with changes in its demographic makeup, the Naval Academy is slowly integrating more interpretive social sciences into its course work, in the hopes of enhancing its understanding of diversity at home and abroad.

This chapter investigates the focus of the Naval Academy on engineering and its ambivalence toward qualitative studies and anthropology, by first taking into consideration the history and tradition on which the academy was founded. This analysis then leads into a discussion of the current education and training program and the means professors use to integrate studies of the "other" into their course work. To understand fully the dichotomies that exist at the Naval Academy, such as the focus on quantitative as opposed to qualitative studies, on military versus academic, and on training versus education, it is imperative for this chapter also to define Navy culture as a subculture of the United States; that is, as a community which is guided by a set of shared meanings.

This chapter takes as its premise that all people are part of a dominant culture, that is, a system of attitudes, values, dispositions, and norms (Robbins 1999), which affects their behavior and activities. The dominant culture is not exclusive, but rather affects and is affected by other cultures, dominant or subdominant, that move through time in and out of its system, carried by individuals with varying backgrounds and world experiences. Culture in this chapter is thus seen as rather dynamic.

Subcultures are a strong power in the development of U.S. culture as they subvert homogeneity and preserve and enhance U.S. political goals and interests. Subculture here refers to a culture that stands as both a part of and apart from the dominant culture. Members of subcultures focus on and elaborate upon specific norms, values and attitudes and in their minds, enhance those aspects of the dominant culture.

Anthropologists study culture (and subculture) in meaningful, organized ways, by observing detail, by participating in the culture at hand, by comparing their findings to other cultures, and by using theory to comprehend in its fullest a particular worldview, system of behavior, belief, and psychology. In today's world, social scientists are quick to generalize in global terms, thereby ignoring the individual case or "averaging" it into oblivion (Wolf 1974:91). (It is perhaps how politicians have failed to acknowledge the real threat of terrorism in a timely manner.) Anthropology, furthermore, understands the hidden dynamics of a culture, that is, the "network" of social relations and the "fabric" of human culture (Wolf 1974: 93). Anthropology acknowledges the "adaptive qualities" of social links and subcultures as well as their "resistance to change" (Wolf 1974:93). An anthropologist thus will understand subcultures as interacting with and, on some level, mirroring the dominant culture in a dynamic manner.

This chapter understands Navy culture as a fluid and slowly changing subculture of the United States. Given the ever-fluctuating context and pressures of the U.S. dominant culture, such as terrorism and war; and inner social events, such as the focus on equal opportunity and diversity; the Navy is impelled to respond to and reflect changing dynamics. This chapter ends with a discussion of the developing needs in a developing Navy culture and the place for courses, such as anthropology, in light of external and internal dynamics.

A Brief History of Cultural Studies at the U.S. Naval Academy

The U.S. Naval Academy in Annapolis was founded in 1845 as The Naval School, when the U.S. federal government endorsed the recruitment of naval officers (Karsten 1972:5). In 1850 The Naval School officially became the United States Naval Academy, a four-year military (Navy) college, integrating practical training with academia. It was not, however, until 1933 that midshipmen received a bachelor of science degree at graduation. Women were not admitted until 1976, when Congress authorized the admission of women to all service academies.

From the start, the Naval Academy was technically oriented, though some courses in the humanities and social sciences were offered. French focused strictly on the learning of proper grammar; the literature used in the 1850s and 1860s was *La Vie de Washington*, that is, a text on our first president rather than on a French subject. Geography included the study of influences of physical causes on man and the study of countries' natural productions, commerce, manufactures, and governments and naval and military strengths. Courses in history and political science focused on the American government. A book entitled *How to Be a Naval Officer* (Stirling 1940) described the importance of science and technology in the training of future officers. As to English, history, and government, at the time a single department, the author states: "The emphasis placed in this department on such subjects as literature and after-dinner speaking may seem surprising to you, but their importance is great. A naval officer is a representative of his country. He is, wherever he goes—China, Chile or Timbuktu—an emissary of the United States.... He must be articulate; for as a leader he must be able to communicate his orders and ideas forcefully.... A study of history helps to develop what we have called his trained initiative. A study of government gives him an understanding and appreciation of the country whose safety is in his hands" (Stirling 1940: 78). It appears that at this point in the history of the Naval Academy's curriculum, the humanities and social sciences were seen as important for mere "after-dinner" conversation and for the appreciation of other countries. Their study was appreciated as superficially enhancing the diplomatic mission, rather than as contributing complex information and concepts necessary for intercultural communication and understanding. Even language studies were given mere lip service. In 1940, the study of

French, Spanish, German, and Italian were considered beneficial to "the midshipman's general culture" and as opening doors if he desired to qualify as a naval interpreter (Stirling 1940: 83). The curriculum at USNA tends to reflect the political and social concerns of the U.S. government. As the catalog points out: "The development of the Naval Academy has reflected the history of the United States. As our country has changed culturally and technologically, so has the Naval Academy. In only a few decades, the Navy has moved from a fleet of sail and steam-powered ships to a high-tech fleet with nuclear-powered submarines and surface ships and supersonic aircraft. The Academy has changed, too, giving midshipmen the up-to-date academic and professional training they need to be effective naval officers in their assignments after graduation" (USNA catalog 2001–2002:9). Thus, depending on the needs of the Navy, as decreed by the U.S. government, midshipmen study specific courses. The Navy, with its heavy reliance on technology, has thus required technically skilled workers. Engineering has been a major component to the midshipmen's training, although it may be argued that officers, leaders of the Navy, require more interpersonal skills than they do engineering skills.

By 1961, USNA had added to its course offerings many more in languages and cultures. The languages included more than USNA offers today: In 1961, the courses entitled "Language Studies" offered French, German, Italian, Portuguese, Russian, and Spanish, with particular emphasis being placed on oral drill and development of the ability to think and converse in the language. In history, a few courses did not actually focus on the United States and Western Europe. Their titles included: "The History of Russia," "Communism: Theory and Practice," "The Far Eastern Relations of the United States," "The History of Latin America," and a "Seminar in Russian Military and Naval Doctrine."

By 1981, given new political concerns, a new list of language courses was devised. Portuguese and Italian were taken off the list, while Chinese was added. By 1993, Chinese was once again dropped, only to be added again in 2001. History and political science in the twenty-first century offer a wide range in topics, including course offerings on China, Japan, the Middle East, Africa, and Russia.

Historically, elective course offerings at the service academies have been a point of contention. New courses tend to stir controversy, whereas maintaining the traditional educational program sets naval administrators and alumnae at ease. According to one Army officer in 1917, "the charm of West Point is that things never change" (Karsten 1972:24). The same may be said for the Naval Academy, with its emphasis on creating "right-thinking naval leaders, not bachelors of art" (ibid.). Tradition and continuity are valued over change, creativity and innovation in the curriculum.

Similarly, flexibility and sensitivity toward the unknown subject matter are considered unscientific and not acceptable components of naval officer training. In studying the enemy, their culture or worldview is rarely studied. Understanding foreign nations from their perspective and not from a U.S. military perspective is and was historically rarely proposed in midshipmen's coursework.

The focus on the U.S. military perspective and purpose pervading the midshipmen's education, resulted in not only an ignorance of foreign cultures' worldviews, but also in a distancing of military officers from civilian America. In fact, according to Karsten (1972:26), "academy authorities did what they could to make the midshipman conscious of his other-worldliness." The authoritarian military culture stood in stark contrast to the civilian world, with its ideals of egalitarianism and democracy. As one midshipman in the nineteenth century remarked, "My military imagination rarely permits me to recognize, or rather, to realize, the existence of such an order of beings as civilians" (p. 27). Because of the traditional military program, to this day, midshipmen feel academically and socially different from their civilian peers attending liberal arts colleges. In one interview, a midshipman remarked: "I go to college parties and there is very little I have in common with other college students. We find little to talk about." Midshipmen are observers, not full participants of mainstream U.S. society.

The Current State of Affairs

Generally speaking, every midshipman today does take courses in the humanities and social sciences. As the program description states: "Every midshipman's academic program begins with a core curriculum that includes courses in engineering, science, mathematics, humanities and social sciences" (USNA catalog 2001–2002:10). However, such general statements are deceiving. In reality, what is meant by humanities is English and possibly, but not necessarily, language studies. What is meant by social science is a course or two in history, political science, and economics. Within these departments, students focus on American government, international relations, United States history, Western civilization, and civilization and the Atlantic community. As is evident by this list, if midshipmen take only core courses in the humanities and social sciences, they may never encounter societies other than those of Europe and the United States in their four years as students. And yet most naval officers find themselves traveling to a variety of countries, including Japan, the Philippines, and countries in the Middle East and Africa.

If a midshipman chooses to major in either political science or history, she or he will find the opportunity to study non-Western societies. One or two courses in each department are offered on Africa, China, Japan, the Middle East, and Eastern Europe. Excluded are India, Australia, New Zealand, south east Asia, and minority populations, to mention a few. Only in the English Department, Foreign Language Department and the Ethics Department are women's issues periodically a focus of investigation.

From 1994 to 1996, anthropology was taught in the Department of Naval Leadership Ethics and Law. The course was entitled "The Psychology of World Cultures" and was initially greeted with enthusiasm by the students. However, halfway through the semester, students began to complain about the workload, which consisted of two exams, a paper, and a presentation. The requirements were no less stringent than those of other humanities and social science courses. Regardless, responses included: "Well, isn't anthropology a *soft* science, and easy for that reason?" Anthropology's connotation at USNA of being a soft and even easy science says much about midshipmen's attitudes toward and value of studying foreign societies.

When asked to describe their understanding of anthropology, midshipmen rarely make the connection between culture and anthropology. Most understand anthropology to be equivalent to archaeology or the study of human origins. Some have expressed that while they have no idea what anthropology is, they would be interested in it. Fortunately, by the end of the anthropology course that was offered, students confirmed its positive impact on their lives as officers in training, saying it opened their eyes to the complexity of the world around them.[1]

Instead of regularly offering an anthropology course at USNA, some professors integrate anthropological concepts into their courses. Professors who specialize in specific countries often use native materials to give an insider's view. Courses in language studies go even further, by presenting native materials, including literature, film, and song, in the native tongue. In advanced Russian, for example, students approach topics from Russian culture during the Stalinist period to contemporary Russian youth culture by studying classical literary treatment of the theme in Russia, journal and newspaper articles, biographies, poetry, music, and film. Native guest speakers representing the subculture under investigation are invited, and students are encouraged to interview Russians outside class for research projects. In the summer, intermediate and advanced students are encouraged to participate in language studies abroad. Thus, while officially anthropology is not frequently seen in the listing of course offerings, unofficially some anthropology prevails.

The Navy: A Subculture of the United States

While it is unlikely that a naval officer would openly speak against the worthiness of studying foreign cultures, he or she may undermine the study in other ways. This hypocrisy is related to the understanding of the existence of both an official, public culture and an unofficial, internal culture. What is said publicly is not always acknowledged internally. Let us take, for example, the notion of "political correctness" (PC). In civilian America, this term refers to respect and sensitivity toward the values and lifestyles of others, even when these do not coincide with one's own. For the Navy, PC has two applications. As one officer described: "For the authorities in the Navy, it is acting so as not to attract undue attention. For the rest of the Navy, PC is acting as told by authorities" (Fujimura 1999:57). PC in Navy culture is completely different from PC in the civilian world.

As we have seen, historically naval officers were trained to view themselves as superior to the civilian world. This view stems from the list of core values (honor, courage, and commitment) to which officers in training swear, which may differ from the values of civilians born and raised in the United States. Moreover, these values, spoken or unspoken, often contrast with those of mainstream America; thus the Navy may be considered a subculture of American society. Values or, specifically, core values in the Navy are continuously reinforced in daily activities, training, and education of officers. In fact, the core values are at the forefront of training and education. According to one officer: "This . . . emphasis on core values is not isolated in recruit training, but has penetrated every rank and school of Navy culture" (Etnyre 1997:58). From enlisted to officer training, core values are continuously reinforced.

At the Naval Academy, an entire program is dedicated to the midshipmen's moral training. Woven into the core courses is the academy's commitment to "the moral development of its midshipmen and to instilling the Naval service core values of honor, courage and commitment" (USNA catalog 2001–2002:66).

To this day, values training and moral development are openly acknowledged as unique to the Naval Academy experience: "The integrated character development program is the single most important feature that distinguishes the Naval Academy from other educational institutions and officer commissioning sources" (USNA catalog 2001–2002:66). This emphasis on "value training" is quite different from the education of a civilian and, in fact, is seen as a quality that separates or even elevates the naval officer from the rest of civilian America. As one article in the *Navy Times* makes clear: "Values training is part of virtually every step in the process of turning civilians into sailors" (Etnyre 1997:57). According to this statement, one cannot simply be a sailor or an officer one must become it through special socialization.

It is the defining of specific Navy values and the intensity with which they are entertained that distinguishes military culture from civilian culture. Moreover, the lack of diversity in values is also pronounced. According to officers themselves: "[T]he flag and officer corps can be described as being of a 'military mind,' holding a set of values that reflect a more common base among their own ranks than with elected officials" (Etnyre 1997:60). However, no matter how hard the Navy attempts to inculcate the core values, others may prevail. According to one study: "Everything which comes from a military source does not necessarily derive from its character-istics as a military source. Military men are also Frenchmen and Americans, Methodists and Catholics, liberals and reactionaries, Jews and antisemites" (Huntington in ibid.:54). An officer brings with her- or himself other iden-tities that contain but are not limited to those of gender, religion, education, ethnic background, and personal experiences prior to the military.

Finally, the Navy as a whole often appears as a culture separate from main-stream America in that some unspoken values appear to be un-American. As I have pointed out in a recent article: "While naval officers are in many ways 'American,' they also hold values and abide by rules that are unlike values and rules held by other U.S. citizens and, moreover, maintain principles and lifestyles that may even conflict with those of the general American public" (Fujimura 1999:55). When it comes to academics, the value placed on diver-sity is less evident than at civilian colleges.

In an article printed for the October 2001 issue of the University of Chicago alumni magazine, the author states that one important and contin-uous project in keeping students at the university is the enhancement of mul-ticultural events and studies. Everyone is encouraged to express their individual backgrounds and to learn more about others. At Stanford University, the handbook makes clear the impact of the diversification of the United States on campus life and the benefits diversity brings to academic pursuits. Professor Harry Elam, Christensen Professor at Stanford University, explains: "I think there's nothing better in a classroom than to find some-body has brought something new to a text that I have read ten or twelve times. And being open and receptive to that as well as being able to provoke them, to bring that out of them, and to allow a space in which a variety of views can be heard: It's a challenge and it remains a challenge each time we enter the classroom" (Elam 2002). This diversification of the student body is viewed as a natural outcome due to the diversification of the United States, and, while it brings with it challenges in the classroom, it is viewed as important and beneficial to all.

Liberal arts colleges regularly include some discussion of the role of diversity on campus. Even Bowdoin College, a small liberal arts college in Maine with 13.6 percent students of color, challenges its students to grow personally "by constant contact with new experiences and different ways of viewing the world" (Bowdoin College 2002). At the College of Agriculture, Consumer and Environmental Sciences, the website includes a section on Diversity Programs. It states: "The College of ACES seeks to encourage diversity and multiculturalism among its faculty, staff and student body" (ACES 2002). It does so with specific goals, which include increasing diversity among the student body, to create a college environment that values differences among students, faculty, and staff, and to strengthen communication with other colleges.

In contrast, individual expression and personal differences are not a focus in the military environment, even at the academy. As one officer describes: "The naval person has much more of a group ethic than the individual American has. It is quite clear that the military is in many ways on the one hand quite socialistic. On the other hand, we're much more authoritarian than the average American would like. We're closer to a Chinese-Communist model" (Fujimura 1999:58). In this quote, the officer compares his understanding of the Chinese communist political system to that of the Navy, wherein "party" members "work not to aggregate the political will of the people, but instead to carry out the political will of the masters or officers, as the case may be. The naval officer corps functions to carry out the decisions of the Navy leadership and not to elicit the opinions of individual members. In this sense, it is a complete antithesis of Western political ideals of self-determination and democracy" (ibid.).

This worldview makes academics at the U.S. Naval Academy an interesting dilemma. On one hand, midshipmen are being trained to blend into the Navy culture, and, on the other, the professors of the humanities and social sciences are demanding they go beyond what they are told and question what they read. It is no wonder, then, that the Naval Academy has embraced the more objective sciences in the curriculum, offering only a bare minimum of courses in the humanities and social sciences and not offering those courses most likely to celebrate individual and cultural difference.

An ambivalence toward difference has made life for minorities a challenge in the Navy. Minority groups, while openly acknowledged by the members themselves, are not officially recognized as subgroups and may therefore be classified as unofficial culture groups within the Navy. This is due to a commonly upheld myth that the Navy is colorless and classless, and distinction and privilege are based on ability and experience.

In reality, a person's color, family background, and gender are important to a military member's identity and how the person is viewed by others (Fujimura 1999:60). Since 1942, the military composition has tried to reflect that of the general American social makeup. Among the enlisted, this effort has resulted in African Americans currently being overrepresented, which is not, however, true among officers, where "all minority racial or ethnic groups have been underrepresented (or unrepresented)" (Etnyre 1997: 9). This underrepresentation or even nonrepresentation of ethnic and U.S. racial diversity in the military mirrors the lack of integration of diverse subject matters, specifically those of multiculturalism and gender, for example, in the education of military officers. It appears that the military does not value cultural diversity, either in practice or in thought. It is as if the goal of the academy in the nineteenth century—to make midshipmen aware of their superiority—is still a part of the unspoken belief system, only at this time, standard texts have been replaced: Edward Freeman's *General Sketch of European History*, used at the academy in the late nineteenth century, which was "an exercise in nation-ranking by 'racial' characteristics . . . (and in which) 'Aryan' nations were ranked above 'semitic,' oriental and African states" (Karsten 1972:35), is no longer part of the required reading.

On the other hand, some are not treated as equal to their peers, even though equality within the ranks is put forward as a goal. To this day, women continue to struggle for equality and fairness. In a study on women at USNA during their first year of integration in 1976, it was found that women were not going to be accepted as equals easily. However, it was surmised that as more women entered USNA the men would become less resistant to the integration, simply through contact. According to the author: "[E]xposure to women as peers at USNA did tend to break down stereotyping and traditionalism" (Durning 1978:vii). However, even with more women at the academy today—albeit they make up only 10 percent of the total enrollment—the struggle for female equality there continues. While life for female midshipmen continues to improve, women feel they still need to prove themselves to receive equal treatment.

Equality and difference are not mutually exclusive terms, and while one might seek equal and fair treatment, one's uniqueness remains a feature people everywhere may be proud of. As a minority at the Naval Academy, a person is likely to join unofficial groups to gain support for hr or his uniqueness. African American women feel more of a mutual bond within the Caucasian-dominated naval culture, simply because of their shared identity. As one informant remarked: "Whereas we might have completely different social backgrounds, we still identify with one another, simply because we are black." The only organizations that do support African Americans include clubs such as the USNA's Black Midshipman Club, which meets once a semester to listen to guest speakers and to watch films. Other meetings may occur in church, choir practice, and during sports events (Fujimura 1999).

An important aspect to academia is the right to voice one's thoughts. While naval officers pride themselves in defending the United States, a country that stands for, among other things, freedom of speech, in the naval community the exercise of the freedom to speak one's mind is not feasible. A member is allowed to voice her or his opinion only when asked to do so by an authority. Officially, one can speak only when specifically addressed or called upon. This attitude becomes a problem in the context of the social science classroom, where individual thoughts and ideas are necessary for a productive academic experience. In fact, perhaps the biggest issue professors face at the academy is teaching the students to think for themselves. Engineering appears to be a much more user-friendly major for a midshipman, since it does not ask for as much subjectivity as it does demand objective, learned reasoning.

Current Needs

The events of September 11, 2001, made the military stop to ponder the consequences of not understanding the enemy and the necessity of doing so. Military personnel and civilian faculty received phone calls regarding language and cultural course offerings at the Naval Academy. More than ever, it seemed midshipmen wanted more courses in the humanities and social sciences. But it is not just the terrorist threat that has sparked an interest. Over the past ten years, the makeup of the Navy itself has changed, as more women and ethnic minorities are joining. Suddenly there is a need to be sensitive to different cultural needs within the Navy.

As we have seen, the focus of the Naval Academy curriculum historically has reflected the needs of the Navy as well as political and social events. During the Cold War, studies of communism and the Soviet regime were integrated. Students studied the Russian language in order to understand the enemy. Given this tendency, as the Navy realizes the urgency of developing deeper cultural understanding both at home and abroad, there is hope for more cultural sensitivity.

How exactly the U.S. Naval Academy will respond to both external and internal changes remains to be seen. However, as long as anthropology is understood to be a synonym for archae1ology or as useless to the training and education of midshipmen, it most likely will not be integrated. The likelihood that the Naval Academy will ever include Anthropology as part of the corps curriculum is slim in view of the fact that traditionalists continue to view advances in technology as the only means to end hostility toward the United States.

Note

1. Comments leading to this statement were recorded in course evaluations.

References Cited

ACES. 2002. "Introduction to ACES." Available at: www.aces.uiuc.edu. Viewed June 2002.

Bowdoin College. 2002. "Student Affairs." *Bowdoin On-Line Course Catalog.* Available at: www.bowdoin.edu. Viewed June 2002.

Durning, K. 1978. "Women at the Naval Academy: The First Year of Integration." Research report, Navy Personnel Research and Development Center, San Diego, CA.

Elam, Harry. 2002. "Introduction to the Humanities." Available at: www.stanford.edu/teach/handbook. Viewed Spring 2002.

Etnyre, R. 1997. "Naval Leadership and Society." Master's thesis, Naval Postgraduate School of Monterey, CA.

Fujimura, C. 1999. "Official and Unofficial Culture: The U.S. Navy." In *Problems and Issues of Diversity in the United States.* Larry Naylor, ed. Pp. 55–67. Westport, CT: Bergin and Garvey.

Karsten, P. 1972. *The Naval Aristocracy.* New York: Free Press.

Robbins, Richard H. 1999. *Cultural Anthropology: A Problem Based Approach.* Ithaca, NY: F. E. Peacock Publishers.

Stirling, Y. 1940. *How to Be a Naval Officer.* Camden, NJ: The Hadden Craftsmen.

Wolf, E. 1974. *Anthropology.* New York: Norton & Company. USNA Catalog 2001–2002.

CONCLUSION

Anthropology and the U.S. Military

Pamela R. Frese

T he textbook I use when I teach "Introduction to Anthropology" successfully illustrates the rich holistic perspective of our world for my students (Haviland 2002). In particular, this text asks students to consider the role that the United States plays in world affairs. In the chapter that introduces facets of linguistic anthropology, Haviland describes how the lexicon in American Standard English is devoted to words that reflect American society and cultural beliefs:

> English is richly endowed with words having to do with war, the tactics of war, and the hierarchy of officers and fighting men. It is rich, too, in militaristic metaphors, as when [Americans] speak of 'conquering' space, 'fighting' the 'battle' of the budget, carrying out a 'war' on poverty, making a 'killing' on the stock market, 'shooting down' an argument, or 'bombing' out on an exam, to mention just a few. An observer from an entirely different and perhaps warless culture could understand a great deal about the importance of warfare in [Americans'] lives, as well as how we go about conducting it, simply from what we have found necessary to name and how we talk. (Haviland 2003:401).

Indeed, anthropologists have spent a great deal of thought on the role of warfare within a variety of societies, including the origins of war in prehistoric and nonhuman primate communities and in non-Western, "primitive" groups. Several scholars continue to pursue these more traditional lines of inquiry in new directions (Carneiro 1994; Goldschmidt 1997; Reyna and Downs (eds.) 1994; Rosaldo 1993; Wrangham and Peterson 1996; see Simons 1999 for an excellent review of social science research on warfare). Recent anthropological perspectives include scholars whose research explores foreign militaries and modern war (Ben-Ari 1998; Lomsky-Feder and Ben-Ari [eds.] 1999; Stewart 1991; Warren [ed.] 1993; Winslow 1997). Others consider the important dimensions of modern war and peace (Gusterson 1996; Hawkins 2001; Rubinstein and Foster [eds.] 1997) and reflect on the impact of war and militaries on the civilian victims (Moon 1997; Taylor 1999; Zur 1998). And anthropologists have made significant contributions to understanding the military as an institution and a set of cultural beliefs and practices within U.S. society (Harrell 2000; Lutz 2002a,b; Simons 1997).

Forensic anthropologists have worked with the U.S. military in a variety of ways since at least 1948 (Giles and Hutchinson 1991; Giles and Vallandigham 1991; Hinkes 2001; Hoshower 1999; Neep 1970; Snow 1948; Webster 1998). In addition, "anthropometrics are used to design everything from fatigues to airplane cockpits. Recently, a lot of these things are being redesigned for the 'new' military" (Heather Edgar, Personal Communication, November 2002) (see also "Anthropometrics":www.mt. wsmr.army.mil/mtd-oe-human-factors.html).

Obviously, anthropologists have much to contribute to a contemporary understanding of the U.S. military as a social institution and as a set of complex beliefs and practices. But how fine is the edge that anthropologists walk in their field research? On one side "lurks" potential ethnocentric bias due to our embeddedness in our own cultural constructs, and on the other side, the siren's call to "go native." Going native takes on another meaning for anthropologists who work with the U.S. military. We balance between a sympathetic stance in support of the military and its goals and how much we choose to support a non-military view as representatives of the victims of war or of the oppressed within military institutions. This carefully negotiated position of the anthropologist is really a liminal position, a mediating position between the world of the U.S. military and the perspectives of the surrounding civilian populations and/or one that straddles the worldviews of practicing applied military anthropologists and that of participants in academic anthropology. As Anna Simons points out in chapter 6 in this volume, anthropologists "straddle two slippery slopes" and must constantly be aware of "power flows and the extent to which anthropologists get caught in them." Positions of liminality can be dangerous, but they also can engender power; anthropologists can provide important perspectives on modern war and on the use military force. Anthropologists also can contribute to sustained world peace through critical understandings of the role of the U.S. military in the world. As Simons so perceptively asks,

> Does anyone know where our policies of intervening only in certain places (like Somolia and Kosovo) but not others (such as Liberia) might lead? Perhaps the vantage point from which we view war today is really a precipice, and in trying to pierce the fog of others' wars, we have lost sight of the edge on which we ourselves teeter. . . . most who read this . . . have been lucky; we have escaped war's tornado-like fury. Not so those who cannot read this or anything else because their lives have already been dominated, disrupted, shattered, or ended by armed conflict. . . . As anthropologists, how should we respond? (Simons 1999:96).

Taking a different perspective on the U.S. military, Catherine Lutz provides an excellent overview of the 20th century militarization process and the hegemonic role that is played by the U.S. military in world affairs. In particular, Lutz argues that, traditionally, "anthropological thoughts turned on how to write less imperial ethnographies, but not ethnographies of imperialism" (Lutz 2002b:732) and that too few anthropology students "were confronted with the idea of the U.S. imperium, of global militarization, and of the cultural politics that make its [the United States] wars seem either required of moral persons or simply to be waited out, like bad weather. These missing pieces of anthropological knowledge have only now come home to roost with great urgency" (ibid.). Lutz's work and that of the contributors to this volume illustrate the diverse and important contributions that anthropologists can and should make to world peace and to an understanding of the U.S. military.

And the U.S. military needs anthropologists to help understand diversity within and outside of the military institution and the implications this understanding may have for successful military ventures, especially those that promote peace and understanding across national boundaries. Anthropologists must recognize the need to engage a powerful social institution like the U.S. military and to propose a variety of ways in which our strengths in understanding social institutions and cultural beliefs and practices can apply to crucial issues in the modern world. This is equally true for practicing anthropologists interacting with various parts of the U.S. military and for those of us who teach the value of holistic anthropological perspectives to students who, we hope, will develop more critical perspectives on our modern world.

References Cited

"Anthropometrics." 2002. Available at: www.mt.wsmr.army.mil/mtd-oe-human-factors.html. Viewed on November 10, 2002.

Ben-Ari, E. 1998. *Mastering Soldiers: Conflict, Emotions and the Enemy in an Israeli Military Unit*. Oxford: Berghahn.

Carneiro, R. L. 1994. "War and Peace: Alternating Realities in Human History." In *Studying War: Anthropological Perspectives*. S. P. Reyna and R.E. Downs, eds. Pp. 3–27. Langhorne, PA: Gordon & Breach.

Giles, E. and D. L. Hutchinson. 1991. "Stature- and Age-Related Bias in Self-Reported Stature." *Journal of Forensic Sciences* 36(3): 765–780.

Giles, E. and P. H. Vallandigham. 1991. "Height Estimation from Foot and Shoeprint Length." *Journal of Forensic Sciences*, 36(4): 1134–1151.

Goldschmidt, W. 1997. "Inducement to Military Participation in Tribal Societies." In *The Social Dynamics of Peace and Conflict: Culture in International Security*. R. A. Rubinstein and M. L. Foster, eds. Pp. 47–65. Dubuque, IA: Kewndall/Hunt.

Gusterson, H. 1996. *Nuclear Rites: A Weapons Laboratory at the End of the Cold War*. Berkeley: University of California Press.

Harrell, Margaret C. 2000. *Invisible Women: Junior Enlisted Army Wives*. Santa Monica, CA: RAND Corporation.

Haviland, William A. 2003. *Anthropology*. 10th ed. Belmont, CA: Wadsworth.

Hawkins, John Palmer. 2001. *Army of Hope, Army of Alienation: Culture and Contradiction in the American Army Communities of Cold War Germany*. New York: Praeger Publishers.

Hinkes, M. J. 2001. "Ellis Kerley's Service to the Military." *Journal of Forensic Sciences*, 46(4): 782–783.

Hoshower, L. M. 1999. "Dr. William R. Maples and the Role of the Consultants at the U.S. Army Central Identification Laboratory." *Journal of Forensic Sciences*, 44(4):689–691.

Lomsky-Feder, E. and E. Ben-Ari, eds. 1999. *The Military and Militarism in Israeli Society*. Albany: State University of New York Press.

Lutz, Catherine. 2002a. *Homefront: A Military City and the American 20th Century*. Boston: Beacon Press.

——. 2002b. "Making War at Home in the United Sates: Militarization and the Current Crisis." *American Anthropologist*, 104(3):723–735.

Moon, Katharine H. S. 1997. *Sex Among Allies: Military Prostitution in U.S.–Korea Relations*. New York: Columbia University Press.

Neep, Wesley A. 1970. "Procedures Used by the U.S. Army to Ensure Proper Identification of the Vietnam War Dead and Their Acceptance by the Next-of-Kin." In *Personal Identification in Mass Disasters*. Thomas Dale Stewart, ed. Pp. 5–9. Washington, DC: National Museum of Natural History. The Smithsonian Institution.

Reyna, S. P. and R. E. Downs, eds. 1994. *Studying War: Anthropological Perspectives*. Langhorne, PA: Gordon & Breach.

Rosaldo, R. 1993. "Introduction: Grief and a Headhunter's Rage." In *Culture and Truth: The Remaking of Social Analysis*. R. Rosaldo, ed. Pp. 1–21. Boston: Beacon Press.

Rubinstein, R. A. and M. L. Foster, eds. 1997. *The Social Dynamics of Peace and Conflict: Culture in International Security*. Dubuque, IA: Kewndall/Hunt.

Simons, Anna. 1997. *The Company They Keep: Life Inside the U.S. Army Special Forces*. New York: Free Press.

———. 1999. "War: Back to the Future." *Annual Review of Anthropology*, 28:73–108.

Snow, Charles Ernest. 1948. "The Identification of the Unknown War Dead." *American Journal of Physical Anthropology*. n.s., 6:323–328.

Stewart, N. K. 1991. *Mates and Muchachos: Unit Cohesion in the Falklands*. McLean, VA: Brassey's.

Taylor, Christopher C. 1999. *Sacrifice as Terror: The Rwandan Genocide of 1994*. New York: Berg.

Turton, D., ed. 1997. *War and Ethnicity: Global Connections and Local Violence*. New York: University of Rochester Press.

Warren, Kay B., ed. 1993. *The Violence Within: Cultural and Political Opposition in Divided Nations*. Boulder, CO: Westview.

Webster, A. D. 1998. "Excavation of a Vietnam-era Aircraft Crash Site: Use of Cross-cultural Understanding and Dual Forensic Recovery Methods." *Journal of Forensic Sciences*, 43(2): 277–283.

Winslow, Donna. 1997. *The Canadian Airborne Regiment in Somalia: A Socio-Cultural Inquiry*. Ottawa, Canada: Minister of Public Works and Government Services.

Wrangham, R. and D. Peterson. 1996. *Demonic Males: Apes and the Origins of Human Violence*. Boston: Houghton Mifflin.

Zur, J. N. 1998. *Violent Memories: Mayan War Widows in Guatemala*. Boulder, CO: Westview.

About the Contributors

Pamela R. Frese is a professor of anthropology at the College of Wooster in Wooster, Ohio. Her research and publications include cross-cultural constructions of gender, the anthropology of religion, and symbolic anthropology. She specializes in complex societies, especially Mexico and the United States.

Clementine Fujimura is an associate professor in the Department of Language Studies at the U.S. Naval Academy. She earned a Ph.D. in cultural anthropology at The University of Chicago in 1993. Research and publication topics include U.S. and Russian military cultures, child abandonment in Russia, and juvenile delinquency.

Jeanne Guillemin is a medical anthropologist whose early work was on maternal and child health. In 1992 she was one of the investigators of the 1979 anthrax outbreak in Soviet city of Sverdlovsk, which she documented in her book, *Anthrax: The Investigation of a Deadly Outbreak* (University of California Press, 1979). A professor at Boston College, she is also a senior fellow at the MIT Security Studies Program and, for 2002–2003, a fellow at the Dibner Institute for the History of Science and Technology.

Margaret Harrell is a senior social scientist at RAND, a nonprofit research organization. She received her doctorate in cultural anthropology from the University of Virginia, where her work focused on gender, class, and race theory as they explained the experiences of Army spouses. Her research expertise is in areas of manpower and personnel, military families, and military quality of life. Her current research includes studies of military spouse employment, management of general and flag officers, future officer career management, and the feasibility and advisability of sabbatical leaves for military officers.

John P. Hawkins is Professor of Anthropology at Brigham Young University. He has served as an officer in the U.S. Army Reserve, having attained the rank of Lieutenant Colonel before retiring. During his annual tours of duty, he worked with the Walter Reed Army Institute of Research, interacting with, critiquing, and participating in their interdisciplinary social science research on soldier, family, and community life in the U.S. Army. From 1986 to 1988, he did field work in Germany on the U.S. Army enclaves there, and subsequently published *Army of Hope, Army of Alienation: Culture and Contradiction in the American Army Communities of Cold War Germany* (Praeger Press, 2001). Throughout his academic career he also has explored the nature of ethnicity, family, and community among the Mayas and Ladinos of Guatemala.

Joshua Linford-Steinfeld is a doctoral candidate at the University of California, Berkeley, in the program in medical anthropology, a joint program with UC San Francisco. He received a dual bachelors degree in community health and in psychology from Brown University. His research investigates the relationship of weight control and bodily practice to discipline and regimentation; gender and sexuality; and "disordered" eating among men in the U.S. Navy and civilian mental health clinics.

Robert A. Rubinstein is professor of anthropology and of international relations in the Maxwell School of Syracuse University. He holds a Ph.D. in anthropology from the State University of New York at Binghamton and a MsPH from the University of Illinois School of Public Health in Chicago. His research focuses on peacekeeping and conflict resolution and cultural factors in intervention.

Trained as an anthropologist, **Anna Simons** is an associate professor of defense analysis at the Naval Postgraduate School, where she teaches in the Special Operations/Low Intensity Conflict curriculum. She is the author of *The Company They Keep: Life Inside the U.S. Army Special Forces*. Having formerly taught in the Department of Anthropology at UCLA, she now teaches former and future military advisors.

Index